CIVILIZATION OF LOVE

A FAMILY FULL OF LOVE

THE TEACHINGS
OF ST. JOHN PAUL II

"The main current of the civilisation of love runs through the family"
- St. John Paul II

CIVILIZATION OF LOVE

A FAMILY FULL OF LOVE

THE TEACHINGS OF ST. JOHN PAUL II

KATARZYNA DOROSZ

I would like to dedicate this book to all families,
women, men, children and seniors.
May the light of the Church's teaching shape
your hearts, minds and personalities.
Using the words of St. John Paul II and all the Dignitaries
of the Church, I would like to express my gratitude for
bringing the Great Family of the Church to life.

Special thanks to:
– His Excellency Archbishop Christophe Pierre,
Apostolic Nuncio of the United States of America
– Monsignore John Paul Pedrera,
Diplomatic Mission of the Holy See (Vatican)
– Monsignore Séamus Horgan, Deputy Head of Mission,
– Prelate Bogdan Bartołd
– Father Maciej Jaszczołt

They also supported me through their publishing efforts:
Father Dr Adam M. Filipowicz and Father Edmund Szaniawski

I Would like to dedicate this book to my son, Damian.
Through the discovery of the truth about man, may
you enfold everyone in love and peace.
By giving love and support to others, may you find the way to peace.
Bring happiness to others and you will be happy.

Introduction

In many societies, especially in the Western world, there is a dispute about human identity, about the redefinition of marriage and family. Claims are made for the rights of same-sex unions and the ideology of gender is promoted. A traditional marriage, established for centuries as a union between a man and a woman, seems to be seriously threatened today and needs special support. The situation may seem analogous to that in which early Christianity developed in a world permeated by the tradition and culture and pagan beliefs of ancient Greece and Rome. Christian marriages and families, too, although they developed and were formed in the spirit of biblical teaching, especially the theology of St. Paul the Apostle, had to face the difficulties of everyday life far from Christian ideals. As far as specific problems are concerned, the monogamous character of marital relationships, the possibility of remarriage or polygamy, issues of divorce and dissolution of relationships were questioned. Important questions of ethics and morality were raised in connection with promiscuity, adultery or cheating, as well as problems connected with the elderly and lonely, with widows, or in connection with the practice among pagans of abandoning children or aborting fetuses. However, it would be impossible not to address first the question of anthropological foundations, the nature of man as such, and seen in the distinction between man and woman. The Synod of Bishops on the Family, which concluded in Rome in the fall of 2015, pointed out in its final document a number of contemporary problems and threats.

A cultural challenge of great importance emerges today from this ideology of "gender" which denies the difference and natural complementarity of man and woman. It portrays a society without gender differences and trivializes the anthropological basis of the family. This ideology introduces educational projects and legislative guidelines that promote personal identity and emotional relationships in complete disregard of the biological differences between man and woman. A person's identity is reliant on individualistic choice, which can also change over time. In the eyes of faith, sexual differences between people bear the image and likeness of God (Genesis 1:26-27). "This tells us that not only is man as such the image of God, not only is woman as such the image of God, but man and woman as a couple are the image of God. The difference between man and woman is not for opposition or subordination, but for unity and procreation, also in the image and likeness of God (...) We can say that without mutual enrichment in this relationship - in thought and in action, in affection and in work, also in faith - two cannot even fully understand what it means to be man and woman. The modern culture has opened up new spaces, new types of freedom, and new depths to enrich the understanding of this difference. But it has also introduced many doubts and much skepticism (...). The removal of difference (...) creates a problem rather than a solution". (Francis, General Audience, April 15, 2015)[1].

It is to be hoped that, just as Christianity gradually transformed the mentality and culture of individuals and entire societies in the first centuries, so it continues to have this potential, which needs to be nurtured and constantly reawakened, in the age of contemporary changes and threats. In order to properly define, understand and develop oneself, man needs reference to permanent, unchanging values and a firm, internally consistent anthropological foundation, both on the basis of philosophy and theology. The teachings of St. John Paul II, whose legacy as a Pope is impressive, including encyclicals, exhortations, letters, homilies, Wednesday catechesis or audiences, are an invaluable help in this regard. How much effort did the Pope put into promoting personalism based on Christianity, defending the dignity of man and woman, defending the dignity of the human person from conception to natural death and promoting and building a «civilization of

---

[1] Synod of Bishops. 14th Ordinary General Assembly, *Final Report of the Synod of Bishops For the Holy Father Francis (October 24, 2015)*, 8, Libreria Editrice Vaticana 2015.

Introduction

love» in the world?[2] For example, suffice to cite a passage from the apostolic exhortation Familiaris consortio [22], where John Paul II emphasizes the equality of man and woman and the role Christianity has played in attributing value to the dignity of both:

The dignity and responsibility of women, equal to those of men, must be emphasized above all. This equality is realized in particular in the gift, proper to marriage and to the family, of oneself to another spouse and of oneself to both children. [...] God bestows personal dignity on man and woman in equal measure, enriching them with the inalienable rights and responsible tasks proper to the human person. [The Apostle Paul will say: "All of you ... through ... faith are sons of God - in Christ Jesus ... There is no longer a Jew or a pagan, there is no longer slave or free man, there is no longer male or female, for you are all one in Jesus Christ." [3]

The following publication, *Civilization of Love. A family full of love*, written by Katarzyna Dorosz, is a kind of compendium of John Paul II's statements on the philosophy and theology of man, marriage and family. After recalling the Pope's biography, selected thoughts of his Mentor (the Blessed Cardinal Stefan Wyszyński, Primate of the Millennium) and interesting facts about John Paul II's life in the chapter *Totus Tuus*, the author presents the Pope's teaching arranged thematically in the following chapters: *Human, Woman, Man, Marriage, Family, Child, Senior*.

In this compilation, through her extensive research Katarzyna Dorosz allows the Reader to get acquainted with the Pope's teaching on a particular topic of interest. She does it so subtly and delicately that she does not subject particular fragments of John Paul

---

[2] It is impossible to list and analyze all of John Paul II's teachings here, but it is also worth remembering his lectures on this subject, which he gave as Karol Wojtyla at the Catholic University of Lublin and which were later reflected in publications translated into other languages: K. Wojtyła, *Osoba i czyn oraz inne studia antropologiczne (Person and Act, and other anthropological studies)*, 3rd ed., Lublin 1994; *Miłość i odpowiedzialność (Love and Responsibility)*, Lublin 2015 (1st ed, 1960); *Rozważania o istocie człowieka, (Reflections on the essence of a human)* Kraków 1999.

[3] Jan Paweł II, *Familiaris consortio. Apostolic Exhortation on the duties of a Christian family in the modern world*, Warszawa 2007, 22, pp. 51-52.

II's teaching to deeper analysis and her own evaluation, but leaves it for personal reflection and assessment of everyone who dares and wishes to read what is not only worth saving from oblivion but also recognizing as truth and making it a basis for teaching and fulfilment in life. Therefore, let this publication be a contribution to the return to the beauty of thought and the richness of the teaching of St. John Paul II and let us undertake our own in-depth study of individual issues, which also go beyond the subject of this book, in order to find answers to important questions that intrigue a contemporary man.

Father Adam M. Filipowicz

Civilization of Love.
A Family Full of Love

Saint John Paul II, known as the Pope of the Family, in his teaching shows the beauty of family, its value and role in building a civilization of love. On the pages of this book we find a simple study of the most important statements of St. John Paul II. They deal with marriage as a covenant of love, talk about the richness of family, about the role of man and woman, about the greatest treasure which is a child, about seniors and relatives. The extended family circle makes it possible to realize the greatest need of the human heart, which is love. A very well-chosen selection of abundant quotations from the Pope's teachings about the family encourages to read and helps to understand what should be done so that life in the family becomes a source of happiness for parents and children. It also contributes to the building of good in the community of the Church and the whole human family.

Father Edmund Szaniawski

Fot. Janusz Gojke

Totus Tuus (All Yours)

In the final years of his life, while suffering from Parkinson's disease, Pope John Paul II did not have the strength to speak, but he found the spirit of God within to guide him. It was in this infirmity that he saw strength.

He never left us alone. Always in love with the Lord, he intended to see his many years of service to humanity to the end.

It is never easy when one is in pain, now imagine the age and illnesses of the Pope and that he never complained. John Paul II received something extraordinary, a strength that allowed him to love God and His people until the very end. And here the question arises: did the life of the Pope have an end at all...?

Non omnis moriar – Not all of me will die

To me, it exemplifies 26 years of service to people and humanity. There was no room for complaint or pain in it.

On the grand scale of things, the Pope referred to the Human Will and urged us to resolve and stand for ourselves. He addressed the Commandment of Love to each individual, warning us against egoism. He suggested focusing on the common good. He said that a human is the only creature in the world that God created like Himself, so by definition they should not characterized by egoism, by materialism, but by readiness to give themselves. Human beings should therefore be guided by morality, responsibility, and the commandments of love.

John Paul II also claimed that *we are sinful and this belongs to the frailty of man, but God does not retain the memory of sins, God loves man and seeks for him true freedom*. Which means that man makes mistakes, but God forgives him.

"Let your spirit come and renew the face of this earth"

Katarzyna Dorosz

You are my protector, my support…
And I am endlessly grateful
That you are with me every day,
and I am with Christ.

Kasia Dorosz

A few words about the Pope from Poland

John Paul II was not only the Holy Father, but also a polyglot, poet, educator, playwright, amateur actor, philosopher and mystic; he was an extraordinary man who drew his strength and greatness from his love for God and His fellow people.

He was born as a beloved child of Emilia and Karol Wojtyła on May 18, 1920 in Wadowice. This hometown shaped the character and heart of the future Pope. When he set out for the Holy See of Peter, he took with him wonderful memories of his family, especially his father. When he was 9 years old, his beloved mother died, and three years later his older brother, Edmund, also passed away. Overnight, little Lolek had to grow up.

Karol's education was personally supervised by his father - he gave him tutoring in the evenings and took care of his spiritual development by going to church with him and teaching him prayers. Thanks to this guidance, Lolek became an altar boy and later became the leader of a whole circle of altar boys. Influenced by his father's teachings and prayers to the Holy Spirit, he later wrote the famous encyclical on the Holy Spirit.

Karol was very talented and eager to learn. After passing his high school exam he went with his father to Krakow, where he began studying Polish philology at the Jagiellonian University and developed his passion for acting. Participation in acting workshops helped him to survive later in life: it reduced his fear, gave him strength and hope, especially when he was left alone in the world.

After the outbreak of World War II, in order to help his father who was beginning to suffer from heart disease, Karol took up a job in a quarry in Zakrzówek and in a water treatment plant in Borek Fałęcki. Although the work was often beyond his strength, he never complained. However, in February 1941, his father died and young Lolek felt very lost. Then Jan Tyranowski, a tailor, helped him find his vocation, and a year later Karol secretly entered the seminary. In the meantime, he also finished his theology degree at the Jagiellonian University.

In 1946 Karol Wojtyla was ordained by Cardinal Adam Stefan Sapieha and was sent to Rome, where he began doctoral studies at the Pontifical University of St. Thomas Aquinas (he obtained his doctorate two years later). After returning to Poland he became the vicar in the village of Niegowici. There he started to teach children, founded a theater for them and went on trips with them. He taught in five schools in his parish. He lived very modestly, because everything he possessed he gave to the poor and the sick.

On August 17, 1949, he returned to Krakow and became the curate at St. Florian's Church. Guided by the principle that *the most important thing is man and the truth about him*, he was involved not only in academic pastoral work and care for the sick, but also in the theater movement. He was recognized for his work and, on the recommendation of his mentor and friend Cardinal Stefan Wyszynski, was elected auxiliary bishop of Krakow in 1958. It was then that he took the words *Totus Tuus* as his motto (All Yours).

In the Vatican, he was valued for his wisdom and his skills as an orator and negotiator. He spoke at the Vatican Council many times. When on June 26, 1967 in the Sistine Chapel the oath of cardinals took place, Karol Wojtyla was among them. And here, for the first time in the history of the Church, universal applause broke out when the then Pope Paul VI put the *Beretta Rosa* on the Pole's head.

Eleven years later, on October 16, 1978, Karol Wojtyla became the Pope. The adoption of the names John and Paul, he explained as follows:

I also adopted the same names as those chosen by my beloved Predecessor John Paul I. For already on 26 August, when he revealed to the Holy College that he wished to be called John Paul - and this duality of name was without precedent in history - I perceived in this a sign of grace on the way of his new pontificate. And since this pontificate has lasted only 33 days, it falls to me not only to continue it, but to take it up again, as it were, at the very point of departure which the choice of these two names testifies in advance. In adopting them, in the footsteps of my beloved Predecessor, I wish - I believe that so did he - to express my love for that particular legacy which Popes John XXIII and Paul VI left and my readiness to continue it, with God's help.

Through these two names and two pontificates I associate myself with the whole tradition of this Holy See, with all its Predecessors, in this twentieth century and in previous centuries, as if in stages, with that continuity of mission and service which marks the specific place of the See of Peter in the Church. John XXIII and Paul VI constitute the stage to which I wish to refer directly, the threshold from which, together with John Paul I in a certain sense, I intend to move forward into the future, guided by that infinite trust and obedience to the Spirit which Christ the Lord promised and sent to his Church.

(The Holy See, John Paul II)

The personal secretary of John Paul II during his entire pontificate was Stanislaw Dziwisz. However, Cardinal Stefan Wyszynski had the greatest influence on the formation of the loving and faithful attitude of the Polish Pope. He participated, among others, in the inauguration of the pontificate, and also joined the *homagium*, the official homage paid to the new pope by cardinals. While he was kissing the papal ring, John Paul II, as a sign of respect for Wyszynski, rose from his throne, kissed his hand and shook it. The next day, a similar event took place during the Pope's meeting with the Poles who had come to Rome. The Primate of Poland and the Holy Father embraced each other in a long hug, after which John Paul II said: *There would not be on the See of Peter this Polish Pope, who today, full of the fear of God, but also full of confidence, begins a new pontificate, if there had not been your faith, not retreating from imprisonment and suffering, your heroic hope, your total entrustment to the Mother of the Church, if there had not been Jasna Góra - and this whole period of the history of the Church in our homeland, which are connected with your bishopric and primate's ministry.* With these words the Pope paid tribute to his mentor. Interestingly, John Paul II later also admitted that he owed his pontificate to Wyszynski. He recalled many times: *I will not forget the words he said to me on October 16 - the day of St. Hedwig of Silesia - as the decision of the conclave was near: 'If they choose you, please do not refuse'. The Primate of the Millennium helped me a lot then. I could answer the question asked to me after the election: 'I accept'.*

As the Pope, John Paul II became the greatest defender of human dignity. He believed that *the value of man does not derive from what he has, even if he possesses the whole world, but from who he is*. He also connected the category of the dignity of work with the concept of human dignity, claiming that human work has an ethical value: *Work is the good of man. For through work man realizes his humanity, becomes more of a man.* He was not afraid of working people, he understood them because he came from among them, with his convictions based on his own experience of hard work in the quarries.

In addition, John Paul II fought for equality for all people, including representatives of different nations and religious denominations. He addressed them with the words: *Do not be afraid! This is our 'to be' and our 'to have'!*, emphasizing that there are no worse or better people or worse or better nations. He loved everyone equally; otherness did not exist for him. He also valued the elderly and encouraged young people to pay special attention to them, so that they would always remember that the elderly are the treasury of life's experiences. He used to say, *old age can be unkind* and he himself endured suffering with dignity, never hiding it and treating it as a part of life.

Karol Wojtyla, Pope John Paul II passed away to eternity on April 2, 2005...

For his extraordinary ministry and his faithfulness and love for God and men, he was first beatified (May 1, 2011) and then canonized (April 27, 2014). He was (and in our minds still is) an extraordinary man who brought love, harmony and faith that never left him, even in the most difficult moments of his life. He proclaimed that *each of us has a purpose and a task in life*. He knew his own perfectly well and fulfilled it. He drew his strength from the balance between contemplation and active life - and he knew how to share it with others.

> The Pope gave people the power to act.
> He had the wisdom and courage to change the world.
> He had the courage to love.
> And for this, we thank him.

From his mentor

In dealing with the reflections of the Holy Father John Paul II we cannot omit a reference to the words of his great friend, mentor and spiritual guide, Stefan Wyszyński, the Primate of the Millennium.

He was an exceptional man who loudly and courageously manifested his faith throughout his life, even in times of persecution. But he died quietly, on the day of the Ascension of the Lord - May 28, 1981. He offered his suffering and illness, as he himself said, for John Paul II, who was lying in the hospital at the time after an attempt on his life. He offered it for the Holy Church and for families. He devoted much attention to the latter issue during his Primate ministry. Since this book deals with the topic of family, it is worth getting acquainted with the views of the Primate of the Millennium on this issue.

We're famous for our patriotism. This is a fact. But perhaps we place too many demands on the Motherland, the Nation, and not enough on ourselves. And yet peace in the Nation flows from peace at home. So often today people speak about maintaining the peace. Peace is made strong in hearts and minds filled by grace and living faith. If it is in the heart, in the thoughts of men, it will certainly manifest itself in the family. If it is maintained in every family, then it will prevail within the borders of our Homeland. There is no other way to strengthen and preserve peace!

Jasna Góra, 15th August 1977

„The order of the heart of every fellow citizen must be connected with the order of the family, for in the family the social order is built. There the national organism is formed, for the nation is composed of families. Therefore, the family, its rights, security and peace must stand at the head of all the duties of social and public life. This is the only way to create a moral and social order, which is based on the principle that everything must be done to ensure that the representatives of the families have adequate living conditions, to safeguard the life of their families from exploitation, deprivation, misery and abuse, and to prevent the needs and duties of family life from being sacrificed for other purposes, especially economic and political ones.

Skałka w Krakowie, 8th May 1978

"We are to be aware of family not only in our home, where father, mother and children live. The family is undoubtedly the most basic unit of social life. Without the family there is no nation, just as without the nation it is difficult to imagine a healthy, orderly state. It is in the family that a nation is born and a sense of social order is nurtured.

Jasna góra, 3rd June 1978

This is your dowry: You yourself and your heart. You are the gift. What you bring will be as you are: pure and clean, or tainted. (...) If you enter into bridal life pure, your marriage will be pure. (...) If you enter stained, everything will be stained.

You know very well how much your family needs your loving heart. But only a pure heart is capable of true love. And you also know well that in order to keep and preserve purity, you must regard it as a treasure and be vigilant not to lose it through carelessness, recklessness or careless stumbling. How do you repair the precious crystal if it falls on the pavement and shatters into tiny pieces? How do you repair the crystal of your heart and body? The blemishes will remain, which is a pity, because the crystal will then lose its value.

And that's why it takes effort, caution and great vigilance to protect your heart, preserve purity and dignity.

A letter to Polish young girls, Jasna Góra, 27th July 1958

The choice of a spouse cannot happen on a whim, a momentary fancy, a passing feeling. The choice must be a careful one, because the future marriage's happiness depends on it. (...) Marriage is not just a matter of the heart, of feelings - it is very much a matter of reason. In choosing a spouse, the laws of God and the good of our Christian faith should play an important role. We must ask whether the person chosen loves God and respects the laws of the Church. This determines whether he or she respects the rights of the spouse. Who is not faithful to God will usually not keep the faith of his spouse. What is more, one must also consider one's own good and that of the other spouse, since people who are good in themselves may not be good for each other, especially when they share differences of disposition, background and upbringing.

Preparation for marriage, 1946

Even Christ the Lord spoke of what is supposed to unite husband and wife. They are to be united by love, and that love is the love that Christ has for the Church. (It is your mutual duty. Not only is the wife to love her husband: the husband is to love his wife. Both of you have hearts, and both of your hearts must be devoted to one another. So you are both being sanctified and perfected by your love for one another.

Surely, this love is stronger when you are younger, because then the qualities of your bodies help you. But the day will come when life will write its wrinkles and heavy marks on your faces. Perhaps the motives that once drove you to mutual affection will be lost. Then, dearest children, other motives will come into play. There arises the duty of mutual life - fidelity. (...) Mutual life is necessary even when the body is no longer attractive; the virtues of the soul and its Christian character must keep you together.

Sermon to catholic spouses, Gniezno, 15th August 1957

"But never, oh my dearest ones, expect help from the other one, but always lend a helping hand yourselves: husband to wife, wife to husband. This will create a proper, truly human, mutual relationship between you.

And never expect too much from the other one, never demand more than you give of yourselves. Always demand more from yourselves. You cannot set things up in such a way that you only make demands on the other party, and release yourself from everything. Only then will there be true love between you, true service and true readiness for sacrifice, when each of you thinks of what is necessary for the other and not for themselves. Only then will there be perfect balance and harmony between you.

And never be in a hurry to make remarks or excuses to each other. It is better to consider first of all „is everything all right in me, am I doing everything that is in my hands". Only when our judgment is positive can we expect good from the other party.

At the wedding ceremony of Halina and Stefan Jurkiewicz, Warsaw, 6th April 1975

"Mutual life is needed even when the qualities of the body no longer attract you; the qualities of the soul and its Christian character must keep you together.

Through mutual respect... Respect for one another (...)

Through mutual patience... And then - patience with yourself. It is the mark of mature, perfect people. Patience is a sign of mutual understanding and understanding of life. (...)

By childbearing... And here is another means of sanctification for mothers, which the Apostle so strongly emphasizes: a woman shall be sanctified by childbearing [cf. 1 Tim 2:15]. Oh yes, for it is a great torment, sacrifice and hardship. It is a pain so great that people want to do away with it to relieve a woman in her maternal duty. This suffering is of great importance. It purifies you, dear mother, and puts you in the presence of God. It reminds you that it is God who is at work in you, shaping a new life, a child of His, to come into the world. Suffering, which people dislike so much, is a necessary part of our personal perfection and sanctification".

Sermon to catholic parents, Frombork, 15th August 1961

"Spouses so often explain that they no longer feel as fond of each other as they did at the beginning of their journey together. Probably the pedagogy of love failed there. They have forgotten that they are obliged to embrace with love the whole life of the other person and to give themselves to him or her. And this is mutual: the

wife gives herself to the whole life of the husband, the husband to the whole life of the wife.

Marriage is mutual help. The teaching of the Church teaches us about it. After all, this is how it began in Eden, when God himself - as the Book of Genesis explains it to us in simple words - perceived that it was not good for man to be alone and that he needed help.

At the wedding ceremony of Halina and Stefan Jurkiewicz, Warsaw, 6th April 1975

Family life is an incredibly meaningful area in which many sacrifices and renunciations are required. Do not think, Children of God, that the fulfillment of marital duties can be free from sacrifice and from your cross. It takes great and many sacrifices.

You fathers must remember that you live not for yourself but for your family, your wife and children. Your abilities, talents and skills, the fruits of your labor are not your property, but the property of your family. Likewise, your wife's work.

Niepokalanów, 9th April 1972

It is necessary to teach a child a noble way of life, to prepare them for life. It is not enough to throw them into the world and say: deal with it! No, parents, your duty and responsibility for your children lasts for many years. It is up to you to mould and educate your child in such a way to get them used to the practicalities of life, so that they are easily able to manage on their own when they become independent.

To fulfill such a great mission, such a solemn task, one thing is needed: sanctification of both spouses. It is not enough that, bound together by the sacrament of marriage, you live side by side. You must now interact with each other as baptized into Christ's Church and united through the sacrament of marriage. You are not only raising your children, you are raising each other. And in this respect there is no difference between the duties of father and mother, husband and wife. (...) The duties are equal, though different for husband and wife. And the effort must be mutual to sanctify each other. It cannot be allowed that the wife is an angel and the husband is Satan; that the wife is bound by the Ten Commandments and the husband is not; that the wife must be sober and the husband can be intoxicated; that the wife must be faithful and the husband if he so chooses. These are all superstitions! The duties are equal in the sight of God, for God is the Father of both husband and wife. He has established commandments for one and for the other.

Sermon to catholic spouses, Gniezno, 15th August 1957

The modern man, as a result of the omnipotence of the technical lifestyle, feels lost. Technicism takes over. Young people are captivated by the development and power of technology, it suits them very well. They are more often in contact with an apparatus, a tool, than with a person, a human being. There are people who spend hours in direct contact with an apparatus, a tool, a machine or a combination of machines. The machine draws the man in completely, demands his absolute attention. And woe betide him if he did not provide this attention. He could then become completely lost, not only mentally but also physically

To the diocesan directors of youth ministry for men, Warsaw, 14th April 1971

To help young people, it is necessary first of all not to give them scorn in the family circle. After all, when going through life children and young people take most from their homes - both good and bad. (...)

To help young people, you have to take care of them outside the home: at school, at work, in their social environment. We cannot be indifferent to what happens to young people at school and in the street, or to their religiousness and morality. (...)

To help young people, one must try to understand them, appreciate their aspirations and desires. Let us not be indulgent, let us be critical. But let's not exaggerate in passing harsh judgments. Instead of blame, let's shed light on young impulses. (...)

Let us also remember that the young generation yearns not only for bread and prosperity, but also for God, the light of the Gospel, and a model that would inspire them to follow.

Let us create opportunities for the young generation to act and to do good. Let them see their brother in every person. Let them learn to help and serve. Let them not make anyone feel inferior or humiliated. Let them develop in themselves a sense of justice and peace. (...) Let them learn conscientiousness and unselfish diligence. (...)

From his mentor

Do not be afraid of Christ, your Helper! Invoke and worship Him boldly, showing Him to your children and youth! For generations to come, Jesus Christ continues to be "the light of the world. He is always the same: yesterday, today and tomorrow! (...) place them in the unfailing hands of the Best Mother of Christ and of ours, the Mother of the Church, Mary, who nourished and brought up the Saviour of the world. (...) After all, in her light grew up the most beautiful model of our time – Blessed Maximilian Kolbe, who gave his life in place of his brother's.

To parents, teachers and older members of socjety, Warsaw,
Ash Wednesday 1972

People say, 'time is money'. I say, 'time is love'. Money is insignificant, but love lasts. Our whole life is worth as much as the love in it.

Jasna Góra, August 15, 1979.

Only eagles glide over the mountains and are not afraid of precipices, winds and storms. You must have something of an eagle in you! An eagle's heart and an eagle's eye on the future. You must harden your spirit and raise it to be able to fly like an eagle over the hills into the future of our Homeland. Then you will be able to soar like eagle through all historical watersheds, winds and storms, not letting yourselves be ensnared by any bondage.

Remember - eagle are free birds because they soar high.

Gniezno, 1966

Finally, I would like to illustrate to one more statement from the Primate Stefan Wyszyński:

"*We can enumerate other people's faults against us, but our faults against others we generally do not see. We will speak of the beam in our own eye later, or never. First we prefer to deal with the speck in our neighbor's eye*".

Unfortunately, these words perfectly reflect the spirit of our times, the widespread savagery and rampant selfishness. Therefore, I have a request to you, my dears: love each other a little more! Talk to each other, surround each other with care, strive for understanding and compromise. Remember, we must respond to the crisis of civilization with a civilization of love! And then the world will certainly be a better place...

Ecce Homo… (Behold, the man)

'This crisis of civilization must be countered by the civilization of love'
(Apostolic letter Tertio millennio adveniente, 1994)

Beginning our deliberations on the civilization of love, we should pay attention to the human and the whole essence of humanity. In his apostolic letter *Mulieris Dignitatem*, the Holy Father wrote that

> '*man is the highpoint of the whole order of creation in the visible world*'.

> "*His Holiness emphasized man's uniqueness by claiming that 'the life which God bestows upon man is much more than mere existence in time. It is a drive towards fullness of life; it is the seed of an existence which transcends the very limits of time: "For God created man for incorruption, and made him in the image of his own eternity" (Wis 2:23)*"
>
> (*Evangelium Vitae*, 34).

In turn, in the encyclical *Redemptor Hominis*, John Paul II expressed the opinion that as God is love, humans are the fruit of this love. A fruit made in the image and likeness of the Lord. He also clearly indicated that no man can live without love:

> "*Man cannot live without love. He remains a being that is incomprehensible for himself, his life is senseless, if love is not revealed to him, if he does not encounter love, if he does not experience it and make it his own, if he does not participate intimately in it. This, as has already been said, is why Christ the Redeemer "fully reveals man to himself". If we may use the expression, this is the human dimension of the mystery of the Redemption*"
>
> (*Redemptor Hominis*).

Let us therefore take a closer look at the essence of humanity as understood by John Paul II.

According to the teachings of the Pope John Paul II, a man or women is a person, meaning a free, self-aware, autonomous being, capable of managing their lives as well as shaping themselves, which is expressed primarily in one's self-awareness and self-determination:

> *"It is through work that man, using his intelligence and exercising his freedom, succeeds in dominating the earth and making it a fitting home".*
>
> (Centesimus annus, 1991).

They are also a dynamic being that develops and creates itself through conscious and free actions:

> *"In this experience man reveals himself as a person, that is as a completely peculiar structure of self-possession and self-control. As this peculiar structure, man reveals himself in action and through action, in deed and through deed. Therefore person and act constitute a profoundly coherent dynamic reality in which the person reveals himself and explains himself through the act, and the act through the person".*

Due to this, humans can possess, shape and control themselves while taking responsibility for their entire life and striving for excellence.

What is perfection? According to the Aristotelian thought, reiterated by St. Thomas Aquinas, perfection is a finished thing, to which there is no need to add anything else. How does this apply to a person? After all, by definition, they should be a perfect being, because they were created in the image and likeness of God. Not completely, though.

A human is a unity and a whole composed of many different elements closely related to each other, mainly a body and a spirit. While the soul constitutes an element of divinity in a human, the body itself can be weak and sinful. Therefore, when we talk about human perfection, we mean the pursuit of it in the moral and spiritual aspect; interestingly, the essence of both these dimensions is love.

"The love which the Apostle Paul celebrates in the First Letter to the Corinthians—the love which is "patient" and "kind", and "endures all things" (1 Cor 13:4, 7)—is certainly a demanding love. But this is precisely the source of its beauty: by the very fact that it is demanding, it builds up the true good of man and allows it to radiate to others. (...) Love is true when it creates the good in persons and within communities; it creates that good and gives it to others. Only the one who is able to be demanding with himself in the name of love can also demand love from others. (...)

The hymn to love in the First Letter to the Corinthians remains the Magna Charta of the civilization of love. In this concept, what is important is not so much individual actions (whether selfish or altruistic), so much as the radical acceptance of the understanding of man as a person who "finds himself" by making a sincere gift of self. A gift is, obviously, "for others": this is the most important dimension of the civilization of love"

(Letter to families, Gratissimam sane).

This demanding love is the basis of man's striving for spiritual perfection.

In the encyclical *Veritatis Splendor*, John Paul II explained that to achieve perfection "means to build this perfection with one's own effort" by undertaking specific actions in accordance with a certain morality.

> *"God willed to leave man in the power of his own counsel, so that he would seek his Creator of his own accord and would freely arrive at full and blessed perfection by cleaving to God"*
>
> (*Veritatis Splendor*).

Therefore, good intention alone is never enough and it must be followed by the right course of action. According to the Pope, a person's work is also a tool for them to improve themselves. In this way, of course, among other things, the laypeople are actively involved cultural in improvement as an essential dimension of the common good. It is this common good that determines the ability to achieve one's own perfection.

The Holy Father also expressed the conviction that the pursuit of perfection is a manifestation of freedom, which "is a special sign of God's image in man" (*Veriratis Splendor*). It is entrenched as if in the very nature of a human - on the one hand, it is a property of their will, but on the other, it is also a constitutive property of the entire personal subject which constitutes the human. This aspect of John Paul II's understanding of freedom was studied, among others, by Piotr Kupczak from the Catholic University of Lublin, who in his work *Freedom of the human person according to Karol Wojtyła* - John Paul II indicates that thanks to freedom, a human "can realize themselves in a way that corresponds to their nature", which means that not only a person, but the whole humanity is affirmed, expressed and fulfilled only through freedom. John Paul II was of the opinion that it was in line with the evangelical truth about freedom.

> "The person realizes himself by the exercise of freedom in truth. Freedom cannot be understood as a license to do absolutely anything: it implies a gift of self. Even more: it means an interior discipline of the gift. The idea of gift contains not only the free initiative of the subject, but also the aspect of duty"
>
> *(Letter to families, Gratissimam sane).*

While still a professor at the Catholic University of Lublin, in his work *Person and Act* (1969) the Pope defined freedom as a person's self-control and self-determination. In doing so, he closely linked the issue of freedom with the phenomenon of the human person, which in a way is the key to his anthropology. For „man truly becomes himself through the free gift of himself..." (Centesimus annus). Man is therefore a person who is the highest form of their nature and humanity. Such a person is an independent being, distinct in human nature, rational and free, existing for themselves, objectively the most perfect in the created world. They have a spiritual life, but at the same time are rooted in the whole reality of creation. Every individual human being expresses themselves in a life that is rational and above all free. For it is the will, or freedom, self-determination, dependence on one's own self, that determines the highest aspect of the person which is morality.

Why is morality so important to John Paul II? Well, in his view:

> "In man himself many elements wrestle with one another. Thus, on the one hand, as a creature he experiences his limitations in a multitude of ways. On the other, he feels himself to be boundless in his desires and summoned to a higher life. Pulled by manifold attractions, he is constantly forced to choose among them and to renounce some. Indeed, as a weak and sinful being, he often does

what he would not, and fails to do what he would. Hence he suffers from internal divisions, and from these flow so many and such great discords in society"

(Redemptor hominis)

Moreover, from the point of view of human freedom the egoistic, individualistic pursuit of utilitarianism, that is, the intense search for maximum happiness, is also dangerous. According to Pope John Paul II, it can be:

'(...) a "utilitarian happiness", seen only as pleasure, as immediate gratification for the exclusive benefit of the individual, apart from or opposed to the objective demands of the true good.

The program of utilitarianism, based on an individualistic understanding of freedom—a freedom without responsibilities—is the opposite of love, even as an expression of human civilization considered as a whole. When this concept of freedom is embraced by society, and quickly allies itself with varied forms of human weakness, it soon proves a systematic and permanent threat to the family"

(Letter to families, Gratissimam sane, 1994).

However, according to the Holy Father, the awareness of this weakness in a person is not all that can threaten them in the spiritual aspect, because also:

"The development of technology and the development of contemporary civilization, which is marked by the ascendancy of technology, demand a proportional development of morals and ethics. For the present, this

last development seems unfortunately to be always left behind. Accordingly, in spite of the marvel of this progress, and despite authentic signs of man's greatness, signs that in their creative seeds were revealed to us in the Book of Genesis, as early as the descriptions of man's creation (cf. Gn 1-2), this progress cannot fail to give rise to disquiet on many counts. The first reason for disquiet concerns the essential and fundamental question: Does this progress, which has man for its author and promoter, make human life on earth "more human" in every aspect of that life? Does it make itself "worthy of man"? There can be no doubt that in various aspects it does. But the question keeps coming back with regard to what is most essential -whether in the context of this progress man, as man, is becoming truly better, that is to say more mature spiritually, more aware of the dignity of his humanity, more responsible, more open to others, especially the neediest and the weakest, and readier to give and to aid all"

(Redemptor hominis, 15).

Why is it so important to look for God in one's life? The Holy Father explains:

"The man who wishes to understand himself thoroughly-and not just in accordance with immediate, partial, often superficial, and even illusory standards and measures of his being must with his unrest, uncertainty and even his weakness and sinfulness, with his life and death, draw near to Christ. He must, so to

speak, enter into him with all his own self, he must "appropriate" and assimilate the whole of the reality of the Incarnation and Redemption in order to find himself. If this profound process takes place within him, he then bears fruit not only of adoration of God but also of deep wonder at himself"

(Redemptor hominis, 1979).

The Pope's words are confirmed in the Holy Scriptures, which are a great record of this search for and finding of the Creator. One of them is the purity of heart, which John Paul II referred to many times during his speeches.

What did the Holy Father say about purity of heart?

"To have a pure heart is to be a new man, restored by Christ's redeeming love, to live in communion with God and with all creation - that communion which is his original destiny".

"[In this way] purity of heart is [to each] man a task. He must constantly make an effort to resist the forces of evil, those acting from without and those from within - [the forces] that want to tear him away from God. And so a constant struggle for truth and happiness takes place in the human heart. To be victorious in this battle, man must turn to Christ".

"Proclaim to the world the 'good news' of purity of heart and make your life an example of the message of the civilization of love".

"In your lives, do not be afraid to oppose the popular opinion and ideas contradictory to God's law. The courage of faith costs a lot, but you cannot lose love! Do not be enslaved! Do not be seduced by delusions of happiness for which the price is too great to pay, the price of often incurable injuries, or even broken lives [your own and others']!".

"Only a pure heart can fully love God! Only a pure heart can fully accomplish the great work of love that is marriage! Only a pure heart can fully serve another. Do not allow your future to be destroyed. Do not let the riches of love be taken from you. Defend your faithfulness; the faithfulness of your future families that you will establish in the love of Christ".

(Asunción, 18.05.1988)[1]

Purity of heart as the Pope understands it, is associated with faith and love and allows us to understand and judge people in the right way.

'Man must be measured by the measurement of his "heart" (...) Man must therefore be measured by the measurement of conscience, by the measurement of the spirit open to God'.

(Holy Mass For University Students, 1979).

Spirituality and spiritual values were a very important aspect in all of the Holy Father's writings and speeches, as he believed

---

[1] Own retranslation from Polish sources: http://www.mateusz.pl/jp99/pp/1999/pp199906_12a.htm and https://www.fronda.pl/blogi/o-wierze-modlitwie-zyciu/jan-pawel-ii-o-czystosci-serca,23492.html, accessed on: 15.09.2021

that they are an innate need of every human being. They are what distinguishes humans from other creatures. He regarded the abandonment of the search and respect for spiritual emancipation as the source and manifestation of man's personal destruction. John Paul II considered not only material goods, but also some social and cultural conditions of our time as obstacles in the way of opening people's hearts to spiritual values (*Novo Millennio Ineunte*).

In his study *Spirituality according to John Paul II,* Father Marek Chmielewski points out that the contemporary understanding of the concept of spirituality differs from the one presented by the Holy Father. The term has come into general use as a term applied to all higher psycho-emotional states. They can be identified either as states of *altered consciousness* (W. James), or as *peak states of consciousness* (A. Maslow). According to the American Psychological Association, spirituality is considered to be one of the five domains of wellbeing. Therefore, this is not the approach understood and popularized by Pope John Paul II.

John Paul II argued that the essence of spirituality is to be found in truthfulness, that to say in conformity to truth. It is revealed not only in thought or consciousness, but also in human action, which is an important dimension of work. The real immanence of the spirit, understood as the spiritual element in a person, should also correspond to all manifestations of human spirituality.

"The spiritual element in man (as a person) consists in a perceptible way of the conviction expressed in the awareness that *a man acts* and that *something happens inside a man* - what beautiful and wise words by Father Marek Chmielewski.

Therefore, Pope John Paul II spoke about spirituality in connection not only with love or freedom, but also with culture, respect for human dignity and human rights, the need to improve social conditions or the need for world peace.

He also placed great importance on silence as the appropriate atmosphere for contemplation, and at the same time the basis for an appropriate development of the spiritual life.

In his letter *Salvifici doloris*, he wrote that suffering *is also a call to reveal the moral greatness of man, his spiritual maturity*. According to John Paul II, properly processed suffering confirms the great dignity of a human being: it makes them become a completely new person and gives them a new measure for their entire life and vocation. Thus, in a way, they are obliged to achieve inner maturity, understood as human maturity and multi-faceted spiritual maturity. It was characteristic of the Pope to refer in the context of maturity, to both human (personal) and spiritual levels, because, in his opinion, on the one hand human maturity is the *sine qua non* of spiritual maturity, and on the other hand spiritual maturity completes personal maturity.

According to the Holy Father, a human must be seen as a communal being, even though each person is also an individual. As he said:

"Each man exists in all the unrepeatable reality of what he is and what he does, of his intellect and will, of his conscience and heart. Man in reality has, because he is a "person", a history of his life that is his own and, most importantly, a history of his soul that is his own. Man who, in keeping with the openness of his spirit within and also with the many diverse needs of his body and his existence in time, writes his personal history through numerous bonds, contacts, situations, and social structures linking him with other men, beginning to do so from the first moment of his existence on earth, from the moment of his conception and birth".

(Redemptor hominis).

Therefore, humans in the entire truth of their existence as personal, communal, and social being, are *the first and fundamental way of the Church*, marked out by Christ Himself and invariably leading us through the Mysteries of the Incarnation and Redemption.

In his work based on the Holy Father's reflections, *The Ways of the Church Lead to a Man*, Father Arkadiusz Wuwer wrote that in all spheres of life (social and national) a human must always be an end, not a means, a subject, not an object, a starting point, not a pitstop on the way to the finish line. Moreover, the fundamental criterion for the resolution of all kinds of problems should be respect for each person and their dignity. '*For there can be no common or universal good which is not based on the good of a human person - the good of a specific human being*'. John Paul II agreed with these words and claimed that:

"Man (...) is the primary and fundamental way for the Church (...). For this reason the Church is justified in its concern about ensuring that human life becomes ever more human, so that everything that comprises such life corresponds to genuine human dignity.... For the situation in the world today is far removed from the demands of moral order, justice and social love - man lives in constantly increasing fear"

(Redemptor hominis)

The principle of Christian personalism (which Father Wuwer writes about) emphasises the dignity of a human being, also as the source of other principles. It reminds us that a human as a person is the subject and the center of society, which means that in a way they "take priority before society". The purpose of society is to create, through its structures, organizations and functions, conditions which will allow the greatest possible number of individuals to develop their abilities and satisfy their desire for perfection and happiness.

> *"God does not doubt man. Therefore we as Christians cannot doubt man, for we know that man is always greater than his errors and transgressions"*
>
> (Apostolic Letter on the occasion of the Fiftieth Anniversary of the Beginning of the II World War, 1989)

For this very reason the Church must never cease to emphasize the dignity of the person, while opposing every form of slavery, exploitation or manipulation that can be carried out to the detriment of human beings - and not only in the political or economic spheres, but also in the ideological, cultural or medical ones. For human life, according to the Pope, must be ever more human and in keeping with human dignity. And the Church must remember this.

There is another very important issue concerning humans. In his apostolic letter *Mulieris Dignitatem*, the Holy Father wrote:

> *"man is the highpoint of the whole order of creation in the visible world; the human race, which takes its origin from the calling into existence of man and woman, crowns the whole work of creation; both man and woman are human beings to an equal degree, both are created in God's image. This image and likeness of God, which is essential for the human being, is passed on by the man and woman, as spouses and parents, to their descendants: "Be fruitful and multiply, and fill the earth and subdue it" (Gen 1: 28)"*
>
> (Mulieris Dignitatem).

With these words, John Paul II drew attention to the equality between men and women and their unique roles in the world. For the Creator has entrusted "dominion" over the earth to mankind, and thus to all men and women, who derive their dignity and vocation from a common beginning.

Note also the following words:

"Man is a person, man and woman equally so, since both were created in the image and likeness of the personal God. What makes man like God is the fact that - unlike the whole world of other living creatures, including those endowed with senses (animalia) - man is also a rational being (animal rationale).[23] Thanks to this property, man and woman are able to "dominate" the other creatures of the visible world (cf. Gen 1:28)"

(Mulieris Dignitatem).

What conclusion can be drawn from this? Well, both man and woman are persons, and therefore '*the only creature on earth whom God willed for himself*'. And since John Paul II did not doubt the uniqueness of a human being understood as a woman and as a man, these are the issues we will look at in our discussion of the civilization of love.

Woman

*"A woman cannot find herself otherwise,
as soon as giving love to the others"*

(Mulieris Dignitatem)

In the previous chapters, equality between human beings - men and women - was emphasized. Now we will take a step further. According to the words of John Paul II in the apostolic exhortation *Familiaris consortio*, women have a special place in the Church of Christ. As the Pope wrote:

"In creating man and woman, God bestows personal dignity in equal measure on each of them, endowing them with the inalienable rights and duties of a human person. In turn, God reveals the dignity of women to the highest degree when he himself takes on the human body from the Virgin Mary, whom the Church venerates as the Mother of God, calling her the new Eve and setting her forth as the model of the redeemed woman. Christ's subtle respect for women, whom he called to follow him and to be his friends, his notable appearance after the Resurrection to a woman before all other disciples, the mission entrusted to women to bring the good news of the Resurrection to the Apostles - these are all signs that confirm Christ's special recognition of women"

(Familiaris Consortio).

Thus, woman was created for man, and man for woman, are a gift to each other, and should see each other as such in each other's eyes. In *Theology of Marriage*, John Paul II wrote that the reception of a woman by a man, his very manner of receiving her, becomes like the first gift - in such a way that by giving herself (from that first moment when in the mystery of creation she was "given" to man by the Creator), a woman at the same time "finds herself" through being received and through the manner in which she is received by a man. She finds herself in her own gift ("through the selfless gift of self") when she is received as the Creator intended, that is, "as and for herself", through her humanity and through her femininity, when in this reception the full dignity of the gift is secured, reaching. She does so through the surrender of who she is, in the pervading truth of her humanity, in all the obviousness of her body and gender, of her femininity, even to her personal depth and to the fullness of self-possession.

The equal dignity of man and woman does not mean being identical with men, as some women often emphasize. In a letter sent to the IV UN World Conference on Woman (May 26, 1995), John Paul II wrote that:

> *"Such an identity would only impoverish women and society as a whole, distorting or destroying the unique richness and intrinsic value of femininity. According to the Church's vision, men and women have been called by the Creator to live in profound reciprocal communion, knowing one another and offering themselves as gifts, working together for the common good and complementing one another through the complementarity of feminine and masculine qualities".*

The woman was therefore given to the man as "a suitable help for him" (Genesis 2:18). Commenting on this phrase, the Pope wrote: *woman is to 'help' man - and at the same time he is to help her - above all in just 'being a man'* (*Mulieris Dignitatem*). In doing so, she explains that becoming or being human consists in "finding oneself" in experiencing the selfless gift of self, which is also the essence of true love. The "humanization" of man, therefore, on the part of woman consists in actualizing in him the capacity to love, and this follows from the fact that "woman cannot find herself except by bestowing love on others" (*Mulieris Dignitatem*).

In his *Reflection on the Apostolic Letter "Mulieris dignitatem"*, Father Marek Chmielewski points to the **meditative nature of women's spirituality**. It is worth mentioning that in his understanding, Christian meditation is a form of prayer which has been attracting more and more interest in recent years, because it is commonly perceived as a counterbalance to the anxieties of modern existence and can bring healing, free the man from everyday stress and give inner peace. Relating this to a woman, he states that one of the peculiar characteristics of her spiritual and religious personality is precisely her natural capacity for meditative relationship to God, man and the world around her.

This is reflected in John Paul II's words about the dignity and importance of a woman's vocation and what can restore it - namely, experiencing love.

"Christ, who knows people's inner self (Lk 16:15; Acts 1:24), responded to women's deepest need to be fulfilled in love with this attitude, for "woman is called from the beginning to be loved and to love. (...) the dignity of a woman is closely tied with the love she receives for her femininity itself and, at the same time, with the love she in turn bestows"

(Mulieris Dignitatem).

It is in this sensitivity of woman to Christ, which the Pope so extensively demonstrated, that the theological foundation of meditative attitude and the meditative dimension of woman's spirituality must be found. It also manifests itself in sensitivity to man, which in *Mulieris dignitatem* was called, probably for the first time in the history of the Church, "a woman's genius". In fact, it can be said that the entire course of the Pope's meditation on the dignity and vocation of woman culminates in this very expression: "a woman's genius". For it defines that special kind of sensitivity of a woman for another person, which only love can enable in man. And therein lies all the enabling power of women.

> *"A woman's moral strength, her spiritual power is connected with the knowledge that God entrusts human beings to her in some special way. Of course, God entrusts each person to all people and to each individual. However, this entrusting applies in a special way to woman, precisely because of her femininity, and constitutes her vocation in a special way. (...) A woman is strong in the consciousness of entrusting, strong in the fact that God "entrusts man" to her always and everywhere, even in the socially disadvantaged conditions in which she may find herself (...) [a woman] becomes an irreplaceable support and a source of spiritual strength for others who sense great spiritual energies within her"*
>
> (Mulieribus Dignitatem).

Thanks to this awareness, this trust, the moral strength of women can be seen in many female characters known not only in Biblical accounts, but also from human history in general.

Returning to the question of the equality of man and woman, including giving oneself to another, it is worth reflectingon words from the Holy Father:

> *"The dignity and responsibility of women, equal to those of men, must be emphasized above all. This equality is realized particularly in the gift attributed to marriage and to the family, of oneself to another spouse and of both to their children. What human reason*

alone can sense and know is fully revealed by the Word of God. The history of salvation is in fact a continuous and glorious testimony to the dignity of woman"

(Familiaris Consortio).

These words are also consistent with the message of Pope Paul VI, who said in one of his speeches:

"In Christianity, more than in any other religion, woman has from the beginning had a special status of dignity, whose numerous important aspects are revealed in the New Testament.... It is clear that women must participate in the living and active structure of Christianity in such a way as to bring out those of their capabilities which have not yet manifested themselves.

The time is coming, the time has already come, when the vocation of the woman is fully realized. The time when a woman radiates her influence on society and acquires a power never before possessed. Therefore, at a time when humanity is undergoing such profound changes, women imbued with the spirit of the Gospel can be of great help to humanity so that it does not fall"

(Mulieris Dignitatem).

Therefore, the role of a woman in "saving" the modern world and man and her responsibility for this mission are beyond dispute. The importance of the woman in society and the Church has been repeatedly exposed in the speeches of John Paul II.

"In our era, advancements in knowledge and technology are making it possible to achieve previously

unknown levels of material prosperity for some, which unfortunately brings with it the marginalization of others.

In this way, this one-sided progress can also bring a gradual loss of sensitivity to human beings, to what is essentially human. In this sense, above all, our time is waiting for the revelation of that "genius" of woman which will secure sensitivity to man in every situation; because she is man! And because "love is the greatest "

(1 Cor 13:13) (Mulieribus Dignitatem)

For in the Spirit of Christ every woman can discover the full meaning of her femininity, and thus become, as it were, a selfless gift to others and at the same time find herself. As the Holy Father wrote,

"Through a remarkable juxtaposition in the Letter to the Ephesians, it becomes fully explicit what constitutes the dignity of a woman both in the eyes of God the Creator and Redeemer, and in the eyes of humans: man and woman. Here, based on God's eternal plan, woman is the one in whom the order of love in the created world of persons finds its first root. The order of love belongs to the inner life of God Himself, to the Trinitarian life. In the inner life of God, the Holy Spirit is the personal hypostasis of love. Through the Spirit, the uncreated Gift, love becomes a gift to created persons. This love, which comes from God, is given to creatures: "the love of God has been poured out into our hearts by the Holy Spirit who has been given to us" (Romans 5:5)"

(Mulieris Dignitatem)

It is therefore clear from the Holy Father's words that the calling into existence of a woman alongside a man to form a unity, allows God's love to pour into the hearts of beings who have been created in his image and likeness. By calling Christ the Bridegroom, the Church and the Bride, we can also see this analogy as an indirect confirmation of the truth of woman as bride. The Bridegroom is the one who loves. The bride, on the other hand, is loved: she is the one who experiences love in order to love back. The Pope emphasizes that *the dignity of a woman is closely tied to the love she receives for her femininity and, at the same time, with the love she in turn bestows.* In this way, the essential truth about both person and love is confirmed.

By saying that the woman is the one who must experience love in order to love back, John Paul II had in mind not only this specific spousal arrangement of marriage, but a more universal scope, marked by the juxtaposition of woman in relation to the totality of human relationships, in various ways defining the coexistence and interaction between people, namely men and women. He believed that

> *"In this broad and multifaceted context, the woman has a special value as a person, and at the same time a specific person who is a woman has particular personal value because of her femininity. This applies to all women and to each individual woman, irrespective of the cultural context in which she lives, irrespective of her spiritual, psychological or physical characteristics, such as age, education, health, work, marriage or celibacy"*
>
> (*Mulieris Dignitatem*).

The value of a woman's vocation is also linked to her ability to sacrifice herself for others, to give of herself to them on a daily basis. At the Fourth World Conference on Women in Beijing (June 29, 1995), John Paul II expressed the following opinion:

"It is by sacrificing herself for others every day that a woman expresses the deep calling of her life. Perhaps even more than a man, she sees the human condition because she sees him with her heart. She sees him regardless of various ideological or political arrangements. She sees him in his greatness and in his limitations, and she tries to meet him and help him. In this way, in the history of mankind, the basic plan of the Creator is fulfilled, and in various ways He continuously demonstrates the beauty - not only physical, but above all spiritual - with which God has endowed man, and especially woman, from the beginning".

"If the right of access to various public tasks is to be granted to women in the same way as it is to men, society must at the same time create such structures that married women and mothers are not in practice forced to work outside the home, and that their families can live with dignity and prosper even when a woman devotes herself entirely to her own family.

It is also necessary to overcome the mentality that it is more honourable for a woman to work outside the home than within the family. This requires, however, that men esteem and love women with all respect for their dignity, and that society create and develop conditions conducive to domestic work"

(Familiaris consortio)

The Pope also addresses the issue of women's work within the family and emphasizes its importance and weight.

"This work should be thoroughly valued. The toil of every woman connected with giving birth to a child, with its nursing, feeding and upbringing, especially in the first years, is so great that no professional work can match it"

(Gratissimam sane).

Father Piotr Kroczek draws attention to two postulates made by the Holy Father to legislators. The first is that work in the home should "regain its due understanding within the current labour law". And according to the second postulate, maternity should be understood "as a sufficient entitlement to an adequate remuneration, necessary to support the family in this very important phase of its existence."

The Pope himself, however, in a letter sent to the Fourth UN World Conference on Woman (May 26, 1995), pointed out that

"The problem facing most societies is to reaffirm or rather strengthen the role of women in the family, while at the same time creating the conditions for them to use their talents in the process of building society and to enjoy their full rights. However, the increased participation of women in the job market, in public life and in general in decision-making processes of social importance on an equal footing with men will continue to pose problems if its cost is incurred by the private sector. The state has a duty to act in this area in accordance with the principle of subsidiarity, which it must implement through appropriate legislative initiatives and

social security policies. In an uncontrolled free market economy, there is little chance that women will be able to overcome the obstacles in their path".

The Holy Father had no doubt that the equal dignity and responsibility of both man and woman fully justify a woman's access to public duties. On the other hand, however, he emphasized that the true advancement of woman, demands an explicit recognition of the value of her maternal and family duties whether in relation to all other public duties or in relation to all other professions. He wrote, among other things, that:

"Moreover, these duties and occupations must complement one another if social and cultural development is to be truly and fully human. This will become easier if (...) a renewed "theology of work" illuminates and deepens the meaning of work in Christian life and establishes the fundamental bond which exists between work and the family, and thus the primordial and inalienable importance of work for the home and for the education of children"

(Familiaris consortio).

Clearly, the Pope paid attention to the special role of women as wives and mothers. Rev. Tadeusz Syczewski, PhD. in his reflections also referred to the work of a woman within the family, as emphasized by John Paul II:

Although the prospects of professional work in society and apostolate in the Church open before a woman, nothing can be compared with the extraordinary

dignity whose source is motherhood, when it is experienced in all its dimensions.
(The duties of the Christian family in the modern world)

Thus, the female personality and the fulfillment of her femininity are most fully revealed in two dimensions: motherhood and virginity. In terms of the family, the former is particularly important. John Paul II wrote that:

"From the very beginning, motherhood includes a particular openness to the new person: it is the woman's lot. (...) This unique way of communing with a new person who is being formed in turn creates a human relation - not only to her own child, but to humans in general - which profoundly characterizes the whole personality of a woman"
(Mulieribus Dignitatem).

To further emphasize the supernatural dignity of motherhood, the Holy Father, using words from the liturgy, declared that:

"the first condition for the respect of the inviolable rights of the human being is the reverence for the mother and the cult of motherhood"
(The duties of the Christian family in the modern world)

The above words can be supplemented by the following statement of John Paul II, referring to the essence of motherhood:

"[the essence of motherhood is] that it refers to a person. It is constituted by that unique and unrepeatable union of persons: mother with child and child with

mother. Even when the same woman is the mother of many children, her personal relationship to each of them characterizes motherhood in its very essence. For each child is born in a unique and unrepeatable way, both for the mother and for the child. Each is uniquely and inexpressibly embraced by that maternal love on which his or her education and growth as a human being are based"

(Redemptoris Mater, 45).

John Paul II, in a letter sent to the IV UN World Conference on Woman (May 26, 1995), also expressed his position on the widespread opinion that motherhood would limit a woman and hinder her ability to function in her private and professional life.

"It is necessary to combat the erroneous view that motherhood enslaves women, that their devotion to family and especially children prevents them from realizing their personal aspirations, and that women as a category are prevented from actively participating in society. It is not only the children but also women and society itself that suffers when a woman is made to feel guilty for wanting to stay at home to raise and care for her children. Rather, the mother's presence in the family, which is so essential to the sustainability and growth of this basic unit of society, should be valued, commended and encouraged in every way".

According to John Paul II, the primary role in raising a child is always played by the mother. Because of the special relationship that binds her to the child, she provides the child with a sense of security and trust, without which it would not be possible to properly form its personal identity and establish healthy relationships with others. This relationship also translates into religious education because it helps to turn the child's heart and mind toward God - long before formal religious education begins. But this mission is so important and delicate that no mother should be left alone to carry it out. Only the presence and care of both parents, as well as the quality of the relationship between them, can properly influence the development and functioning of the child and its relationships with others.

From the above considerations, it follows that the time devoted to the upbringing of a child is particularly precious, since it determines the future of the human person, the family, and even society as a whole. It is also important for peace in the world, as John Paul II reminded us in his message, saying that:

"To educate for peace, a woman must first of all cultivate it within herself. The source of inner peace is the awareness that one is loved by God and the willingness to respond to his love. (...) [Therefore, women] must become peacemakers in all their lives and actions: they must be witnesses, announcers, and teachers of peace in relationships between individuals and generations, in the family, and in the cultural, social, and political life of nations, especially where there are conflicts and wars. May they walk unceasingly on the road to peace, which many women before

them have already embarked upon, bearing witness to their courage and foresight!"
(Message for the XXVIII World Day of Peace, Vatican,
8th December 1994).

As we can see, then, the position of a woman - her dignity and the importance of her vocation, her important role both in the family and in society, her spiritual and moral strength were very often touched upon in the Pope's speeches. He appreciated the "woman's genius", her ability to love and be loved, to give and receive. His words are an extremely precious gift for all women.

Finally, I would like to quote from the apostolic letter *Mulieribus Dignitatem*, in which the Holy Father John Paul II wrote:

"So the Church is grateful for all women and for each individual woman:
- *mothers, sisters, wives;*
- *for women consecrated to God in virginity,*
- *for those who put themselves at the service of so many people waiting for the selfless love of others;*
- *For those who watch over humanity in the family, which is the primary sign of human community;*
- *for women in professional work,*
- *to those who often have great social responsibilities,*
- *to the "brave" women and to the "weak" women - to all women:*
- *as they were conceived by God in all the beauty and richness of their femininity;*
- *as they have been embraced by His eternal love;*
- *just as, together with men, they are pilgrims on this earth, the earthly "homeland" of men, and which often becomes a "vale of tears";*

– how together with man they take joint responsibility for the destiny of humanity, according to the demands of daily life and those ultimate destinies which the human family finds in God himself, in the womb of the ineffable Trinity"

(Mulieribus Dignitatem).

***Repeating after the Pope himself,
Dear Women, we thank you...***

Man

"Happy spouse who he undertakes with the fear of God great gift of wife love and reciprocates him"

(Miłujcie się)

The equality and dignity of man and woman as human beings have been mentioned several times in previous reflections. This is an important issue not only for women, but for men as well. John Paul II repeatedly stressed that only mutual respect and understanding can make their relationship lasting and meaningful.

"Authentic conjugal love presupposes and requires that a man have a profound respect for the equal dignity of his wife: «You are not her master,» writes St. Ambrose, «but her husband; she was not given to you to be your slave, but your wife.... Reciprocate her attentiveness to you and be grateful to her for her love.»[69] With his wife a man should live «a very special form of personal friendship.»[70] As for the Christian, he is called upon to develop a new attitude of love, manifesting towards his wife a charity that is both gentle and strong like that which Christ has for the Church"

(Familiaris consortio).

The Holy Father's emphasis on equality between man and woman also refers to a man's full experience of his own masculinity. His dignity and role as a husband are based on a dialogue of love and the ability to appreciate his wife. The Pope was of the opinion that

"In woman, man finds a partner with whom he can dialogue in complete equality. This desire for dialogue, which was not satisfied by any other living creature, explains the man's spontaneous cry of wonder when the woman, according to the evocative symbolism of the Bible, was created from one of his ribs: "This at last is the bone of my bones and flesh

of my flesh» (Gn 2:23). This was the first cry of love to resound on the earth!"

> *(Message Of His Holiness Pope John Paul II For The XXVIII World Day Of Peace: Women: Teachers Of Peace, 1 January 1995).*

Love, the ability to receive it and to gift oneself to the other person, is what constitutes the essence of marriage, which is based on the bond between a man and a woman. According to John Paul II, women have the unique natural ability to love, but what about men? Are they able to give love or do they only allow themselves to be loved? Well, the Holy Father believed that the ability to love is not exclusively a matter of gender. He said that

> *"To love truly and fully is only possible for one who is capable of 'owning' his soul, of owning himself: owning in order to become 'a gift to others'. Christ teaches us all of this not only by his word, but also by his example"*
>
> *(Homily, Vatican, 24 February 1981).*

In women, this ability is natural, although historically there are known examples of women acting against their femininity and vocation, of women unable to love. Men are taught love – both in terms of accepting it and of giving it. For this reason, John Paul II repeatedly appealed to men:

> *"Husbands, love your wives, even as Christ loved the church and handed himself over for her to sanctify, cleansing her by the bath of water with the word, that he might present to himself the church in splendor, without spot or wrinkle or any such thing, that she might be holy and without blemish. So [also] husbands should love their wives as their own bodies. He who loves his wife, loves himself. For no one hates his*

own flesh but rather nourishes and cherishes it, even as Christ does the church, because we are members of his body. For this reason a man shall leave [his] father and [his] mother and be joined to his wife, and the two shall become one flesh'. (Ephesians 5,25-31)

The Holy Father was also convinced that:

"The second account of creation from the beginning assigns to man the function of the one who primarily receives the gift (cf. Gen 2:23). The woman is from the beginning entrusted to his eyes, to his consciousness, to his sensitivity, to his heart while he is supposed in a way

to safeguard the very process of the exchange of gifts, that reciprocal giving and receiving which, exactly due to that reciprocity, constitutes an authentic communion of persons"

(Theology of Marriage).

Therefore, if in the mystery of creation a woman is "given" to a man, and he, in the whole truthfulness of within her person and femininity, receives her as a gift thereby also endowing her, then in this reciprocal relationship he himself is also endowed – both with the gift of her person and femininity, and with his own gift. The Holy Father emphasized that:

"This masculine gifting - the response to the woman's gift - bestowes the man himself, for in it is revealed, as it were, the distinctive essence of his masculinity, which reaches through all the obviousness of his body and sex to the same depth of "self-possession" by which man is capable both of giving himself and of receiving the gift of the other. Man, then, not only receives the gift, but at the same time is received as a gift by a woman in this revelation, together with all the truth of his body and sex, of the inner, spiritual essence of masculinity itself. The man who is received in this way is in turn mutually endowed by this reception and by this acceptance of the gift of his masculinity. In turn, this reception in which the man finds himself through the "unselfish gift of himself", becomes in him the source of a new and deepening gift of himself to the woman"

(Theology of Marriage).

The exchange described above is therefore reciprocal, and this reciprocity also relates to the self-revealing, increasing effects of this "selfless gift", and the "finding of self".

A man's first role in the family is to be a husband, and his vocation is to the woman who has become his wife. The Pope points out that in God's plan of creation it is the woman who gives new meaning to a man's existence. She is the only one who can fill the emptiness in his life, free him from loneliness, and provide suitable help, and succor to him. In addition, the woman constantly fascinates and surprises the man, her betrothed. Thus, by relating to the woman as wife and mother, the man accentuates his identity and affirms himself as both husband and father. He must be acutely aware of his gift and his vocation, as John Paul II repeatedly reminded us:

"Within the conjugal and family communion-community, the man is called upon to live his gift and role as husband and father. In his wife he sees the fulfillment of God's intention: "It is not good that the man should be alone, I will make him a helper fit for him,"[67] and the makes his own the cry of Adam, the first husband: «This at last is bone of my bones and flesh of my flesh"

(Familiaris consortio).

In his speeches and writings, the Holy Father also showed that through the love for his wife who has become a mother, and the love for his child, a man is capable of naturally understanding and realizing his own fatherhood. And it is this, along with being a husband, that is truly his vocation in life. The Pope wrote that:

"When, in union with the Apostle, we bow our knees before the Father from whom all fatherhood and motherhood is named (cf. Eph 3:14-15), we come to realize

> *that parenthood is the event whereby the family, already constituted by the conjugal covenant of marriage, is brought about "in the full and specific sense". Motherhood necessarily implies fatherhood, and in turn, fatherhood necessarily implies motherhood. This is the result of the duality bestowed by the Creator upon human beings "from the beginning"*
>
> (Gratissimam sane).

According to the Pope, fatherhood involves a great responsibility and care for the family, and an exacting maturity.

> *"'In revealing and in reliving on earth the very fatherhood of God, a man is called upon to ensure the harmonious and united development of all the members of the family: he will perform this task by exercising generous responsibility for the life conceived under the heart of the mother, by a more solicitous commitment to education, a task he shares with his wife, by work which is never a cause of division in the family but promotes its unity and stability, and by means of the witness he gives of an adult Christian life which effectively introduces the children into the living experience of Christ and the Church"*
>
> (Familiaris consortio).

Referring to masculinity, John Paul II drew attention to the weakening of customs and bonds between people, showing that family breakdown is increasingly common. And it is not only about the separation of spouses, but also about the man evading his role as a husband and father, and the neglect or abuse of the family, both physical and psychological. The Holy Father emphasized that:

> "Above all where social and cultural conditions so easily encourage a father to be less concerned with his family or at any rate less involved in the work of education, efforts must be made to restore socially the conviction that the place and task of the father in and for the family is of unique and irreplaceable importance. As experience teaches, the absence of a father causes psychological and moral imbalance and notable difficulties in family relationships, as does, in contrary circumstances, the oppressive presence of a father, especially where there still prevails the phenomenon of «machismo,» or a wrong superiority of male prerogatives which humiliates women and inhibits the development of healthy family relationships"
>
> *(Familiaris consortio).*

Returning to man's responsibility for his family, it is important to point out his traditional role as the person who provides for his wife and children. For many centuries and generations, working to earn money to provide for the family has been one of a man's primary responsibilities. However, according to John Paul II, this widespread opinion was unacceptable because it reduced a man's role in the family only to this duty, and thus confirmed the validity of the absurd saying: «A good father is one who does not get drunk and brings home a lot of money ». Yes, the Pope did not deny that work is necessary, but he was of the opinion that it should not hinder or even prevent a man from fulfilling the many other tasks that he has in relation to his wife and children. And this brings about the reflection that our present reality deviates considerably from this obvious principle.

Preempting the question of why so little content appears in this book section devoted to men, I answer that John Paul II did not pay, unduly more attention to women at all, nor do I, being a woman myself. Simply put, a man's role as the head of the family, as a husband and father, as a human being has been clear and unchanged for centuries. There is no need to fight for it to appear in the social consciousness, to be noticed, or appreciated. Therefore, there is less to convey in this respect, although the content itself is enduring and important. For man is the complement of woman, her bridegroom, one of the dimensions of her vocation. Only the two of them form a unity - divine perfection created in His image and likeness.

Marriage

*Marriage is the way of holiness,
even when it becomes a way of the cross.*

(Homily, Stary Sącz, 16th June 1999)

The family has always been understood as the first, fundamental expression of man's social nature. It is understood in the same way today. It has its origins in the community of marriage, described by the Second Vatican Council as a "covenant". The Holy Father repeated that "in this covenant a man and a woman give and receive one another". Marriage in the sacramental view, then, is a covenant of persons in love. *And love can only be grounded and protected by Love, that Love which 'has been poured into our hearts by the Holy Spirit who has been given to us' (Romans 5:5) (Gratissimam sane).*

And what is love, according to John Paul II? Speaking to the youth, he explained this question as follows:

"To love means to be with the Person one loves (I am with you), it means at the same time: to be with the Love with which I am loved. To love means further: to remember. To walk, as it were, with the image of the Beloved Person in one's eyes and heart. It also means to contemplate this Love that I am loved with and to fathom ever more deeply its Divine and Human greatness. To love means, finally, to be watchful"

(From the address to young people, Częstochowa, 18th June 1983).

The Pope repeatedly emphasized the essence and role of love in the life of man and woman.

"Man cannot live without love. Man remains a being incomprehensible to himself, his life is meaningless unless Love is revealed to him, unless he encounters Love, unless he touches it and somehow makes it his own, unless he finds in it a living participation"

(Redemptor hominis).

According to the Holy Father, a great deal depends on love - both in terms of the life of an individual and of the whole society, nation and even the world.

"There is no happiness, no future for man and nation without love, a love that forgives without forgetting, sensitive to the unhappiness of others, that does not seek its own, but desires the good for others; a love that serves to forget itself and is ready to give generously. We are therefore called to build a future based on love of God and neighbor.
To build a "civilization of love"

(Homily, Sopot, 5th June 1999).

The concept of a "civilisation of love" has not only been accepted in the teachings of the Church but has also become more generally established. The term *civilisation* comes from the Latin word civis, meaning citizen, and emphasises the societal and political dimensions of everyone's existence. However, the deeper meaning of the term is not political at all, but humanistic. In fact, civilization belongs to man's history and corresponds to his spirituality and morality: «created in the image and likeness of God, he received the world from the hands of the Creator with the task of creating it in his image and likeness. In this task and its fulfillment lies the source of civilization, which must be understood ultimately as the «humanization» of the world.

According to papal teachings, marriage is also supposed to constitute an ecclesial community. Its causal agent is the Holy Spirit, who is «the living source and inexhaustible nourishment of the supernatural communion which gathers and binds believers to Christ and one another in the unity of the Church of God». (*Familiaris consortio*). Such a community was even in ancient times rightly called «the domestic Church».

Marriage as a sacrament is celebrated through the words spoken by newlyweds, which in the order of intentionality signify what (or rather: who) the two are determined to be from now on for each other and together. John Paul II, referring to the words: «I take thee to be my wife,» «I take thee to be my husband,» wrote that

these words are at the center of the liturgy of marriage as a sacrament of the Church. The words are spoken by the bride and groom, incorporating them into the formula of a sacramental vow: "I vow to you love, fidelity and honesty in marriage - and that I will not leave you until death do us part". The vow is completed by another vow: "So help me, Lord God Almighty and Triune, and all the Saints". By saying these words, they enter into marriage - and at the same time accept it as a sacrament of which they are both ministers.

(theology of Marriage).

The words of the marriage vow quoted above carry the eternal, yet each time unique and unrepeatable "body language" and set it in the context of a communion of persons. Man and woman become a gift to each other - a gift in their masculinity and femininity - they discover the conjugal meaning of the body, and relate it to each other in an irreversible way, and spiritual in the dimension of the whole of life. According to the Pope,

"The words of the marriage vow declare what constitutes the common good - first of marriage and in turn the family. The common good of the spouses is love, fidelity and honesty, and the permanence of their union until death. This good of both is at the

same time the good of each. It in turn to become the good of their children"

(Gratissimam sane).

John Paul II reminds us that a man leaves his father and mother to be united with his wife (Gen 2:24), which is a conscious and free choice that gives rise to the marriage covenant, and makes a son the husband, and a daughter the wife. Christ in the Gospel, in his conversation with the Pharisees quotes the same words, adding: *And so they are no longer two, but one flesh. What therefore God has joined together, let no man put asunder.* (Mt 19:6). This conscious and free choice is based on love - the nature of marital unity is crowned by the words: *He who loves his wife loves himself* (Eph 5:28). In this way love makes the other one its own self, that is, through love the wife's self becomes in some way the husband's self, and vice versa. John Paul II explained it this way:

"It is a moral unity, conditioned by love and shaped by love. Love not only unites two subjects but allows them to penetrate each other in such a way, spiritually belonging to each other, that the author of the letter can state: "he who loves his wife loves himself". 'I' in a way becomes 'you' and 'you' becomes 'I' (in a moral sense, of course)"

(Theology of marriage).

According to the Pope, the source of all love - marital, parental, communal - is God:

"The Gospel of love is the inexhaustible source of all that the human family as 'communion of persons' nourishes. In love, the whole process of education as the mature fruit of parental love finds support and

ultimate meaning. Through all the hardships, all the sufferings and disappointments which go hand in hand with bringing up a human being, love still passes the greatest test. To pass this test requires a source of spiritual power. That source is invariably found in the One who "loved to the end..." (Jn 13:1).

(Gratissimam sane).

At the same time, the Holy Father adds that:

"The love between a man and a woman in marriage ... is brought to life and sustained by an internal, unceasing dynamism, leading the family to an ever deeper and stronger communion, which is the foundation and principle of the conjugal and familial community"

(Familiaris consortio).

The communion between the spouses is the first to arise and develop. By virtue of the covenant of marital love, man and woman «are no longer two, but one flesh,» and their calling becomes to strive for continual growth in this communion «through daily fidelity to the conjugal promise of mutual total gift.» As John Paul II states:

"This marital communion has its roots in the natural complementarity of man and woman and is strengthened by the personal willingness of the spouses to share the whole program of life, what they have and what they are. Hence such communion is the fruit and sign of a deep human need. In Christ the Lord, however, God accepts this human need, confirms it, purifies it and elevates it, leading it to perfection in the sacrament of marriage"

(Familiaris consortio).

According to this teaching, Love is essentially a gift. And conjugal love, while leading the spouses to a mutual «knowledge» that makes them «one flesh,» does not exhaust itself among the two of them, for it empowers them to the greatest devotion, whereby they become partners with God in giving the gift of life to a new human person. «In this way the spouses, by giving themselves to each other, bring forth a new reality - a child, a living reflection of their love, a permanent sign of marital unity and a living and inseparable synthesis of fatherhood and motherhood» (*Familiaris consortio*).

John Paul II also points out that the communal perspective on marriage requires us to see in a new light the rights and duties of women, the tasks of men as husbands and fathers, and the role of children and the elderly in the family. We must keep in mind that these are not only rights and duties of an organizational, legal or social nature, but also spiritual. The Pope speaks of the need to respect the distinction between the vocation of man and the vocation of woman, and expresses concern for the dignity of women and the essence of fatherhood, which must be understood through his «love for his wife, who has become a mother, and his love for his children. This is where the «grace and requirement for an authentic and profound spirituality of marriage and family» comes from. (*Familiaris consortio*).

The Pope also points out that from this love, understood as an essential dimension of marital spirituality, flows hospitality and openness to others. Thus, it must be understood:

> *"What an important role spirituality plays in the family. Attending Mass together, praying in the evening, praying the rosary together. The adherence to common values that become the foundation of the family"*
>
> (*Theology of marriage*).

In addition to sharing of values, family prayer is also essential to marital spirituality, drawing "its original content from family life itself" and being a mutual witness to the faith that is deeply rooted in the daily lives of the spouses, their children and even others outside the family.

The papal encyclical *Humanae vitae* allows us to construct an outline of marital spirituality. According to its message:

"It is that kind of spirituality in which - by taking into account the "biological" order and at the same time the chastity supported by donum pietatis - the inner harmony of marriage is formed, linked to what the encyclical calls the "dual function of the sign". This harmony means that the spouses communicate with each other in the inner truth of the "speech of the body".

This bond that exists between this "truth" and love is inviolable. The Holy Father also explains this concept:

"The gift of reverence which the Holy Spirit inspires in spouses has a great significance for these "signs of love", because it goes hand in hand with a capacity for profound affection and admiration, a disinterested concentration on the "visible" and at the same time "invisible" beauty of femininity or masculinity - and finally: a profound sense of unselfish bestowal on the "other"
(*Theology of Marriage*).

In his study *Spirituality according to John Paul II*, Father Marek Chmielewski indicates that the result of this spiritual power of marriage and family in the social dimension is its spiritual sovereignty, while its derivative value is the spiritual power and strength of the nation. This is confirmed by the Pope's own words, according to which:

> "A nation that is truly sovereign and spiritually strong is always composed of strong families: families conscious of their vocation and mission in history. At the center of all these matters and tasks there is always family"
>
> (Gratissimam sane).

As is well known, John Paul II often used two phrases in the context of families and especially marriage, referring to different but related issues. The first, more general is the **civilization of love**, and the second, more specific - **responsible parenthood**. He called the Hymn to Love from St. Paul's First Letter to the Corinthians the great charter of the civilization of love. He emphasized that

> *It is concerned not only with individual manifestations (of both egoism and altruism), but above all with accepting the definition of man as a person who 'realizes himself' through the selfless gift of himself. The gift is - of course - the gift to others, "for others": this is the most important dimension of the civilization of love.*
>
> (Gratissimam sane).

It will not be a great discovery to say that man is not sufficient for purely functional relationships. He needs interpersonal relationships which reach deep into his inner self, and which express a totally selfless gift of self. Among such bonds, fundamental role is played by relationships within the family, especially between spouses and between parents and children. The Holy Father pointed out that:

> "A whole immense network of human relationships is born and continually reborn thanks to that bond by

which a man and a woman recognize that they are made for each other and decide to unite their paths, forming one community of life: 'For this reason a man leaves his father and his mother and unites himself with his wife so closely that they become one flesh'" (Genesis 2:24).

One flesh! It's hard not to see the full power of that expression! In the biblical sense, the word "flesh" does not mean merely the physical nature of man, but his entire spiritual and bodily identity. The spouses form not just a community of bodies, but a true unity of persons. It is a unity so profound that they become in temporal reality a reflection, as it were, of the divine 'We' of the three Persons of the Trinity"

(Sermon at the Mass for the Jubilee of Families,
15th October 2000).

It is worth mentioning here that the Second Vatican Council, thoroughly concerned with the question of man and his calling, proclaims that: "the marital union, the biblical 'one flesh' (una caro), cannot be fully understood and explained except in terms of "person" and "gift". Every man and woman is not fully realized except by the selfless gift of self." John Paul II, in his letter to families (*Gratissimam sane*), completes this message as follows:

"The moment of marriage union is the most special experience of this gift. Man and woman, in all the "truth" of their masculinity and femininity, become at that moment a gift to each other. The whole of married life is a gift, but it refers in a special way to this exact moment when the spouses, by giving themselves to each

other in love, bring about the encounter which makes the two of them "one flesh".

The moment of giving oneself to one another in love is also a moment of special responsibility because of the potential parenthood associated with the conjugal act. The Pope emphasizes that:

"At that very moment they may become father and mother, giving rise to a new human existence which in turn takes place in the woman herself. She is the first to know that she has become a mother, and through her testimony the man with whom she has been united 'in flesh' realizes in turn that he has become a father. For this potential and then actualized parenthood, he is responsible together with her"

(Gratissimam sane).

In the light of these considerations, it is easy to see that, according to the Holy Father, marriage carries with it a particular responsibility for the common good, first of the spouses and then of the family. This common good is a human, with the value of a person, a measure of human dignity. Therefore, it is no wonder that John Paul II used the term responsible parenthood, because being a parent means being responsible for new life. From the Pope's teachings, we see that:

"Spouses learn what responsible parenthood is from their own experience and, at the same time, from the experience of other married couples living in similar circumstances, which also makes them more receptive to these teachings. In a sense, then, it is also the case that the "learners" learn "from their spouses" in order

to, in turn, more competently teach each other what responsible parenthood is and how to put it into practice"

(Gratissimam sane).

In doing so, the Holy Father repeatedly pointed out that

"Parenthood creates for itself only the proper coexistence and cooperation of independent persons. This is particularly true of the mother when a new human being is conceived. The first months of its existence in the mother's womb create a special bond which is to a large extent already of an educative nature. (...) The man-father does not take part in this process directly. He should, however, consciously involve himself in the expectation of the child to be born, if possible also at the moment of the child's birth.

For the "civilisation of love" it is essential that the man feels that he has been gifted with the motherhood of the woman, his wife. And this in turn has an enormous influence on the whole process of upbringing. A great deal depends on if and how he participates in this first phase of humanity, whether and how he involves his masculinity and his paternity in the maternity of his wife"

(Gratissimam sane).

The deepest and best defining element of parenthood is, according to the Holy Father:

"paternal and maternal love, which finds in the work of upbringing the fulfillment of a perfect service

to life: parental love becomes, from the beginning, the soul, and thus the norm, which inspires and gives direction to all concrete educational activity, enriching it with such precious fruits of love as tenderness, constancy, goodness, service, unselfishness and a spirit of sacrifice"

(Familiaris consortio).

According to the teachings of John Paul II, upbringing should be understood first and foremost as the bestowal of humanity, and this bestowal is bilateral. The parents bestow their mature humanity on the child, that is, on the newborn, who in turn bestows upon them all the newness and freshness of humanity, that he or she brings into the world. Isn't it right, then, that the Church asks the newlyweds at the time of their wedding whether they want to «lovingly welcome and catholically raise the offspring that God will bestow upon [them]?»

The Holy Father emphasized that marital love is expressed precisely in upbringing as true parental love.

"The communion of persons, which comes at the beginning of the family as marital love, is completed through education and spreads to the children. It is a matter of taking up all the potential richness of each person who grows within a family; it is a matter of not letting it perish or degenerate, but of actualizing it into an ever more mature humanity. And this is also a reciprocal process: the educators-parents are at the same time, in a certain way, being educated. In teaching humanity to their children, they themselves come to know it anew and learn it anew"

(Gratissimam sane).

It should therefore be understood as a mutual interaction - a bestowal of the gift of love and humanity. The Pope adds that:

"Insofar as parents, by bestowing life, participate in God's creative action, they both become participants in His paternal and at the same time maternal pedagogy through education. The Divine Fatherhood - according to St. Paul - is the model for all parenthood in the universe (cf. Eph 3:14-15), and is in particular the model for human motherhood and fatherhood"

(Gratissimam sane).

When referring to marriage, it cannot be overlooked that both love and its covenant must be nurtured. One must respect, accept and listen to each other. To care not only for one's own benefit "me", but also for "us". The Holy Father called this marital dialogue and called for its use by spouses to nurture their love. He wrote, among other things, that:

:In striving to develop an attitude of listening and mutual acceptance that is meant to sustain and develop the love between the spouses, the practice of "marital dialogue" should be undertaken. Through sincere conversation spouses can express their love without judging their partner and without fear of his or her judgment, guided by a just concern for the truth in their mutual relations, showing a tenderness and cordiality that foster dialogue and personal growth and are a source of happiness"

(Letter to Équipes Notre-Dame, 27th November 1997).

According to the Pope, this marital dialogue constitutes:

"a concrete testimony of the mutual marital responsibility that each one accepts in the sacrament: the responsibility to 'be for each other and for their children witnesses of faith and love"

(Lumen gentium).

According to John Paul II, this dialogue leads to deep communion and fosters personal growth. Husband and wife, constantly renewed by His dialogue of love, which allows them to build an authentic relationship, can live in peace and joy fulfilling all their duties (spousal and parental).

"In this way they give convincing testimony, especially to their own children. (...) The welcoming atmosphere of family life, open to all, enables young people to pass through the successive stages of psychological and spiritual maturity"

(Letter to Équipes Notre-Dame, 27th November 1997).

Marital love also has a moral aspect. As the Holy Father pointed out, with the phrase *Husbands, love your wives, for Christ also loved the Church*, Scripture emphasizes this moral duty.

"But in order for such a duty to be recommended, it must be accepted that in the very essence of marriage something of what takes place between Christ and the Church is reflected and realized. It must be assumed that in the very essence of marriage there is contained some part of the same mystery"

(Theology of Marriage).

The words quoted above are very meaningful because they emphasizes the mutual relationship between man and woman in marriage. Marital love involves true unity and selfless giving of oneself to another person. According to the Pope:

"It is a desire born of spousal love which means that the "selfless gift" of the woman must find its response and completion in the corresponding "gift" of the man. Only in this way can both, and especially the woman, "find themselves" as a true "union of two" with respect to each person's dignity. Marital union demands the respect and perfection of the true personal subjectivity of both"

(Mulieribus Dignitatem).

John Paul II emphasizes that:

"[this] gift brings with it a profound and comprehensive concentration on a person - it embraces with this concentration the whole person in their femininity and masculinity - and thus creates an internal atmosphere of personal union. It is only in this atmosphere of personal union that spousal parenthood - the parenthood we call "responsible" - can properly mature"

(Theology of Marriage).

Thus, the logic of the total gift of self to another opens spouses to their potential for parenthood, for in this way they can realize themselves even more fully as a family.

"Obviously, the purpose of the mutual gift between a man and a woman is not only to bear children,

> *but also the mutual continuation of love and life. It is necessary, however, that the inner truth of this gift be safeguarded. Inner does not mean merely "subjective." "Internal" means corresponding to the objective truth of him and her who give the gift. The person can never be a means to an end, a means of "use" - he must be himself the goal of action. Only then does action correspond to its true dignity"*
>
> (Gratissimam sane).

Marriage is therefore both the subject and the object of the gift. For them its most precious gift are children. John Paul II was of the opinion that, according to God's design, *marriage is the foundation of the wider familial community, since the institution of marriage itself and married love are directed at birthing and upbringing the offspring, in which they find their culmination* (Familiaris consortio). The emphasized tis in his speeches and writings:

> *"Happy is a spouse who with humility in God takes up the great gift of his wife's love and reciprocates it. Happy both of them when their marital union is permeated with responsibility for the gift of life which originates in that union. This is truly a great mystery and a great responsibility: to give life to new beings created in the image and likeness of God. Nowhere else does God make himself so radically present to man in his proper action, and nowhere else does he reveal himself so tangibly to man as in his creative action, namely, as the Giver of the Gift of human life"*
>
> (Periodical Miłujcie się, 2005, no. 3).

It is clear to every Christian that without love the family is not a community of persons, *without love it cannot live, grow and perfect itself*. With the Gift of Love, however, another thing is connected - its effect on the human spirit and its inner strengthening. The Holy Father presented it in this way:

"An apostle, when bending his knees before the Father, asks that He 'cause [...] by his Spirit the inner man to be strengthened'" (Eph 3:16). This "strength of the inner man" is at stake in the whole life of the family, especially in all those critical moments when it comes to passing the difficult test of love, the love which the marriage vow expresses in the words: "that I will not leave you until death do us part"

(Gratissimam sane).

It must also be remembered that each human being, each woman and man, has an identity which constitutes the basis of the personal life of a human. It also influences the understanding of marriage as a communion, a covenant. According to the Pope:

"This identity is the capacity to live in truth and love; even more, it is the need for truth and love as a dimension of personal life. This need for truth and love opens man simultaneously to God and to all that exists - it opens him in a special way to the other person, opens him to a life "in communion". It opens man and woman to marriage and the family"

(Gratissimam sane).

In Theology of Marriage, John Paul II addressed the deeply embedded perspective of human existence in the consciousness of humanity. According to Genesis, he stated that both human persons, male and female, were created for marriage: "A man leaves his father and mother and is joined with his wife so intimately that they become one flesh". (Genesis 2,24). For in this way, in his view, a great creative perspective opens up. It concerns an existence that is constantly renewed through procreation (this "self-renewing").

In his work *The Duties of a Christian Family in the Modern World*, Father Tadeusz Syczewski points out that spouses must be well aware that a life of complementarity is a great gift that they wish to give of themselves - according to the words of the Holy Father: *True love is not a vague feeling or blind passion. It is an internal attitude that embraces the whole person. (...) It is a gift of oneself.* This gift is to be for each other in every situation of their lives, in happy and in sad moments, giving the best of themselves.

Christian spouses are apostles not only when they are engaged in the apostolate in the strict sense, but also when they fulfill their duties in their own families in a manner that is appropriate and consistent with their calling. The most important areas of the married apostolate are: raising children, preparing them for their own duties in the family, assisting young married couples, and helping families in crisis, especially those in danger of breaking up. As John Paul II said,

> *"All spouses are called to holiness in marriage according to God's will, and this call is realized as the person is able to respond to God's commandment, animated by a quiet trust in God's grace and in his or her own will"*
>
> (Familiaris consortio).

The Second Vatican Council speaks of the vocation of all the faithful to holiness, specifying that spouses achieve this goal "propriam viam sequentes" - "by walking their own path. Spouses, "by fulfilling their matrimonial and family tasks through this sacrament, imbued with the spirit of Christ which permeates their whole life with faith, hope and love, draw ever closer...to the attainment of their own perfection and mutual sanctification, and thus to the joint glorification of God" (Gaudium et Spes). The Pope also pointed out that:

"One can strive for holiness together as a married couple, and this is a beautiful path, extremely fruitful and important for the good of the family, the Church and society. Let us therefore ask the Lord for an ever-increasing number of married couples who, through the holiness of their lives, will be able to reveal the "great mystery" of married love, which has its origin in creation and is fulfilled in the union of Christ with the Church (cf. Eph 5:22-33)"

(Beatification of Maria i Alozjy Quattrocchi, 21st October 2001).

Given these considerations, and the value of marriage, this indissoluble union of love between two people, cannot be questioned. It must be defended, it must be believed in with absolute conviction. As John Paul II said:

"Whatever difficulties may arise, it is impossible to give up defending that original love which united two people and which God continually blesses. Marriage is a path of holiness, even when it becomes the way of the cross"

(Homily, Stary Sącz, 16th June 1999).

To conclude, I reuse the words of the Holy Father, who left us a wonderful message about marital love.

"Life teaches us that love, marital love, is always a special test of all life. It is not great and true when it seems easy and pleasant. It is when it is confirmed in the trials of life, like "gold in the fire." It would be a very poor understanding of human and married love, if anyone thought that when the time of trial comes, love and joy end. It is then that human affection shows its durability; it is then that devotion and tenderness are strengthened, because true love does not think of itself but of how to contribute to the good of the beloved; its greatest joy is the happiness of those it loves"

(Periodical Miłujcie się, 2005, no. 3).

A husband's prayer for his wife:

Dear God, thank you for my wife. Thank you for her love, femininity, beauty, sensitivity, seeing things from a different point of view. I thank You for our paths that crossed, that we chose each other, and that You blessed our love in the Sacrament of Marriage. Lord, give her patience, understanding, peace and quiet. I give into your care all the difficulties that are between us: arguments, misunderstandings, doubts. Make us a help to each other, help us forgive each other and understand each other better. Please take care of my wife, protect her from evil and give her strength. I want be her supporter and protector. I want to be a husband and father responsible for the upbringing of our children.

I want her to be happy with me. I love her.

A wife's prayer for her husband:

Thank you, Lord, for my husband. For his love, for the good that he gives me. For the fact that through the Sacrament of Marriage we can become one body. I entrust to you, Lord, all his thoughts, gestures, words, decisions and relationships with other people. I entrust to you what I find difficult to love in him, what irritates or hurts me. Lord, bless our love. I pray for faithfulness for him and for myself. I ask for closeness to express and strengthen our love. Help us to always understand each other well, to overcome difficulties, to quell conflicts and to forgive each other. Protect him, Lord, from evil, give him strong faith and holiness. Bless his work. Make him a better husband and father through me.

I want him to be happy. I love him.

Family

The future of humanity comes through family

(Familiaris consortio)

Pope Francis has called John Paul II a witness to the beauty of the family and its inalienable role in society. He also repeatedly refers in his own speeches to his commitment to explaining the meaning and nature of the family as the Domestic Church. The Church in which spouses form a community of persons, and through everyday fidelity to their marital promises, and via the complete and mutual gift of self to each other, they constantly grow.

"Marital and familial community is built on mutual trust. This is the basic good of mutual interactions in the family. The mutual interaction between spouses - and the mutual interactions between parents and children. The deepest foundation of these relationships is ultimately that trust which God himself places in the spouses by creating them and calling them to live in marital and familial community. (...) The family's essence is built on such interactions, on mutual trust, on mutual confidence. Only on this foundation is it possible to build the process of upbringing, which is the fundamental purpose of the family, and its primary function"

(Homily, Wrocław, 21st June 1983).

In his reflections, the Holy Father pointed to the family, based on marriage, as the fundamental building block of society. He said that *in it, as in a safe nest, life develops which must be defended and protected* (Reflection, 1st February, 2004). In his teachings he also referred to the fact that

"The family is (...) the most complete community from the point of view of the human bond. There is no

bond that binds people more closely together than the bond of marriage and family. There is no other which can be so fully described as "communion." Nor is there any other in which the mutual obligations are as deep and comprehensive, and the violation of which more grievously afflicts the human sensibilities of woman, man, children, parents"

(Homily, Kielce-Masłów, 3rd June 1991).

Referring to papal teachings, Father Piotr Kroczek also points out that the rights of the family are based on the principle of its sovereignty and are not merely the sum of the rights of its members. For the family is more than each individual person - it is a community of parents and children, a community of many generations. The Holy See published the 1983 Charter on the Rights of the Family as an expression of this conviction.

The family, according to God's plan, was created as a community of people (spouses, children, elderly, relatives), as a "profound community of life and love," which is also the essence of its mission. It receives from the Creator the mission of guarding, revealing and transmitting love, which itself is also the inner principle, the lasting power and the ultimate goal of this task.

"Love between a man and a woman in marriage and, in a derivative and extended form, love between members of the same family - between parents and children, between brothers and sisters, between relatives and household members - is animated and sustained by an internal, ongoing dynamic, leading the family to an ever deeper and stronger communion, which is the foundation and principle of the marital and familial community"

(Familiaris consortio).

Thus, it is love that animates the interpersonal relationships between individual family members, and it is its inner strength that not only shapes but also strengthens family communion and community.

"To love the family means to know how to value its values and capabilities and to always support them. To love the family means to know the dangers and evils that threaten it so that we can overcome them. To love the family means to contribute to creating an environment favorable to its development. And a particular form of love for the Christian family today, often tempted by discouragement and tormented by growing difficulties, is to "restore its confidence in itself, in its own riches of nature and grace, in the mission entrusted to it by God"

(Familiaris consortio).

In the context of the family as a community, the Holy Father spoke of four types of communion-like relationships in the family: husband-wife, father-mother, son-daughter, brother-sister. This includes emphasizing the dignity and responsibility of woman and the equal dignity and responsibility of man. Family communion should also take special care not only of the spouses, but also of the child. Moreover, it is also meant to stimulate everyone to discover and appreciate the importance of the elderly in the secular and ecclesial community. The whole «domestic Church» is the subject of the preaching of the Word of God, on whose reception, as it were, the life of the Christian family depends. For if it feeds on this Word in its daily life, Jesus Christ is also more fully present in it. In such a community there is an atmosphere of goodness, love, kindness and love of the Savior Himself. Confirmation of this can be found in the words of John Paul II:

> "Since the Christian family is a community whose bonds have been renewed by Christ through faith and the sacraments, its participation in the mission of the Church must be conducted in a communal way: thus together, spouses as a couple, parents and children as a family must live out their service to the Church and to the world. They should be in the faith as "one spirit and one heart", through the apostolic spirit that animates them and through cooperation that involves them in the work of serving the ecclesial and civic community"
>
> *(Familiaris consortio).*

Second Vatican Council also reminds us of this by saying that:

"*the family must share its spiritual riches generously with other families. Consequently, a Christian family, as it arises out of marriage which is an image of and a participation in the loving covenant of Christ and the Church, will reveal to all through the love of the spouses its sacrificial fruitfulness, unity and fidelity, as well as through the loving cooperation of all its members, the living presence of the Savior in the world and the true nature of the Church*".

In addition, according to John Paul II, the Christian family also builds the Kingdom of God in history through the everyday reality that is defined and determined by its living conditions, namely marital and family love.

What integrates communities is not only love, but also friendship, fraternity, hope, mutual help of various kinds, daily provision of good, and exchange of experiences. There is no doubt that a life of love is a joyful message for every human being. Moreover, a person who can truly love and be loved has the capacity to inspire hope in others as well as in themselves. For this reason, the Pope believed, the family will play no apostolic role in the modern world unless it first becomes a place of goodness, hope, love and kindness for its members. A family that is close-knit, animated by a spirit of hope and love, can radiate outwardly by its very example of life, provide the impulse to follow God's commandments. This is why John Paul II asked:

"Families, become what you are supposed to be. You are the living image of God's love: for you have the mission of guarding, manifesting and transmitting that love which is the living reflection and the actual communication of God's love to humanity and of Christ the Lord's love to the Church, his bride"

(Ecclesia in Europa).

According to the Pope's teachings, a Christian family should therefore be a school of the richness of humanity. Richness, as in fullness of its physical, intellectual, religious and moral development. As the "domestic Church," it should introduce the child to a life of faith, and taking responsibility for that faith, it should teach respect for others and responsibility for the Church and the nation. The family is also, as it were, a privileged place for mutual help of different kinds. As John Paul II notes:

"One observes an awareness of the need for closer ties between families in order to provide mutual spiritual and material assistance, a fuller discovery of the Church's mission specific to the family and of its responsibility for building a more just society"

(Familiaris consortio).

The family also has lively and organic ties to society: it constitutes its foundation, constantly supporting it through its mission of service to life. It is *in the family, after all, that citizens are born and find the first school of those social virtues which determine the life and development of society itself.* The family's first and principal contribution to society is therefore the experience of communion and participation in its everyday life. The members of the familial community inspire one another, guided by the "law of selflessness", *which, while respecting and strengthening in everyone their personal dignity as the only reason for value, takes the form of cordial openness, encounter and dialogue, readiness to selfless, generous service and profound solidarity.* In this way, an authentic and mature communion of people in the family is strengthened, becoming the first and irreplaceable school of social life, *an example and stimulus for wider social contacts in a spirit of respect, justice, dialogue and love.* (*Familiaris consortio*).

> *"In the Church, the familial community realizes that it is a small Church by itself, made of sinners who have been forgiven and are walking the path of holiness, finding support in those whom God has joined together in one family"*
>
> (*Letter to Equipes Notre Dame, Vatican, 27th November 1997*)

The family is therefore called to Holiness which the Spirit of God leads it to.

The Pope said that this is reflected in:

> *"(…) the words of St. Paul: 'For all those who are led by the Spirit of God are sons of God' (Romans 8:14). If the Holy Spirit is the soul of the Church (cf. Lumen Gentium, 7), then He must also be the soul of the family, the little domestic Church. For each family unit He must be the inner source of vitality and energy which feeds unceasingly the flame of marital love, expressed in the mutual gift of husband and wife"*
>
> (*Address to the participants in the Plenary Assembly of the of the Pontifical Council for the Family, 4th June 1999*).

But according to John Paul II, in order for the family to evangelize others, it must first draw strength from the Church's liturgy itself - to learn it more deeply in order to live it. "The Domestic Church" should develop a life of prayer within itself, as well as form pathways for the dialogue of Faith. It is the family that should pass on the faith in Christ to the new generations with conviction and joy. For the Pope taught that:

"The family unit should be the first environment in which the peace of Christ is received, nurtured and protected. But in our time, without prayer, it is increasingly difficult for families to carry out this calling. That is why it would be good to return to the beautiful custom of praying the rosary at home, which was prevalent in previous generations. "The family that prays together, remains together"

(Catechesis, 29th October 2003).

In fact, there are few other activities to be done together that have a deeper impact on a family than praying together.

The Holy Father emphasized that:

"Family prayer has its own characteristics. It is a communal prayer of husband and wife, parents and children. Communion in prayer is both the fruit and the requirement of that communion received in the sacraments of baptism and marriage. The words in which Christ promised his presence can be applied in a special way to the members of the Christian family: 'Amen, I say to you, if two of you on earth agree about anything you ask, everything will be given to them by my Father

in heaven. For where two or three are gathered in my name, there am I in the midst of them"
(Familiaris consortio).

Through prayer, the family community invites Christ to be in its midst: spouses, parents and children. When homes become places of prayer, they are at the same time homes «in which families live serenely in the presence of God,» «which share hospitality, prayer and praise of God with their neighbors». The Pope was particularly emphatic on this point:

"The Christian family should stand out as an environment of common prayer, in which the freedom of the sons allows everyone to turn to God and call on Him with the confidential name 'Our Father!'. The Holy Spirit helps us to discover the face of the Father as the perfect model of fatherhood in the family"
(Address to the participants in the Plenary Assembly of the of the Pontifical Council for the Family, 4th June 1999).

The prayer of the family community can also become a place of shared and mutual remembrance, for as the Holy Father wrote,

"the family is a community of generations. It is necessary that all be present in prayer - those who are alive, those who have passed away and those who are yet to be born. Each person must be prayed for in the family to the extent of the good that he or she brings to the family, and family to them. Prayer most fully affirms this good, affirms it as the common good of the family. Prayer also gives rise to this good again and again. In prayer the family finds itself as the first "us" in which everyone is "I" and "you. This is what they are to each

other: husband or wife, father or mother, son or daughter, brother or sister, grandfather or grandchild"

(Gratissimam sane).

John Paul II also pointed out that:

"The family that prays the rosary together reproduces in certain ways the atmosphere of the house of Nazareth: Jesus is placed at the center, joys and sufferings are shared with Him, needs and projects are placed in His hands, hope and strength for the journey are drawn from Him. It is also beautiful and fruitful to entrust to this prayer the children path to growth. It is increasingly difficult for parents today to keep up with their children at different stages of their lives. In a society of advanced technology, mass media and globalization, everything has become so fast-paced, and the cultural differences between generations are increasing. The most unforeseeable messages and experiences are rapidly entering the lives of children and young people, and parents are sometimes anguished as they face the dangers that threaten them. It is not unusual that they experience painful disappointments as they observe the failures of their children who succumb to the delusion of drugs, the allure of hedonism, the temptations of violence, and various manifestations of meaninglessness and despair"

(Periodical Miłujcie się, 2005, no. 3).

The dangers and temptations lurking in the family make it necessary, according to the Pope, to guard the purity of the heart:

> *"It is necessary for the family to stand firm in defense of the purity of its domestic thresholds, in defense of the dignity of each person. (...) Bringing up children to purity is one of the great evangelic duties before us today. The purer the family, the healthier the nation"*
>
> (Homily, Sandomierz, 12th June 1999).

According to the Holy Father, family should also trust in God's help:

> *"Moreover, the dignity and responsibility of a Christian family as 'domestic Church' can be lived only with the constant help of God, which will always be granted if it is asked for in humble and trusting prayer"*
>
> (Familiaris consortio).

Thanks to prayer, the family can be strengthened in its community and communion.

In his work *Duties of A Christian Family in the Modern World* based on the papal teachings, Father Tadeusz Syczewski expressed his belief that every man is responsible for building the communion of people day by day, to the extent of his abilities. This makes the family "a school for a richer humanity." This task is realized especially through grace and love towards children, the sick and the elderly, and above all through the mutual daily service of all family members. The attitude of sharing not only goods but also joys and sorrows plays an important role in this regard. For parents, this is true service: service subordinate to the human and Christian good of their children, enabling them to attain a truly responsible freedom.

In this regard, John Paul II addressed parents with these words:

> *"It is not easy today to create Christian conditions needed for the upbringing of children. You must do everything to make God present and honored in your families. (...) You are the first teachers of prayer and Christian virtues for your children and no one can replace you in this. Preserve religious customs and cherish Christian traditions, teach [your] children respect for every human being. Let your greatest desire be to educate the younger generation in union with Christ and the Church. Only in this way will you be faithful to your parental vocation and to the spiritual needs of your children.*
>
> *Let the welfare of the younger generation be the concern of your life and of your educational work. 'I urge you', says St. Paul, 'to conduct yourselves in a manner worthy of your calling... in order to build up the Body of Christ (Eph 4:1,12). What greater calling can there be other than the one God has given you?"*
>
> (Homily, Łowicz, 14th June 1999).

Through love, respect and obedience to their parents, children in turn also make their irreplaceable contribution to the building of the family. The Holy Father reminded them of this:

> *"Do not be afraid to enter upon the path of your vocation, do not be afraid to seek the truth about yourselves and the world around you. I would so much like all of you to have in your homes an atmosphere of true love. God gave you parents, and for this great gift you*

should often thank the Lord. Respect and love your parents. They gave birth to you and bring you up. They are for you substitutes of God, your Creator and Father. They are, and should be, your closest friends, from whom you should seek help and advice in your life's problems. (...)

Your age is the season of life most favorable for sowing and preparing the ground for future harvests. The more vigorous the commitment with which you assume your responsibilities, the better and more effectively you will fulfill your mission in the future. (...) Truly great is the man who wants to learn"

(Homily, Łowicz, 14th June 1999).

Along with a variety of duties, the daily life of the family also includes the spiritual life, about which the Pope said:

"In everyday life, God calls us to strive for that maturity of spiritual life that consists precisely in living ordinary things in an extraordinary way.

For holiness is achieved by following Jesus, without running away from reality and its trials, but by facing them with the light and power of his Spirit"

(Reflection, 1st September 2002).

In relation to this, John Paul II has told families on more than one occasion to take care of this spiritual aspect of community life:

"More and more individuals and families are taking advantage of vacations to spend a few days in so-called 'Centers of Spirituality' - monasteries, shrines, retreat

houses. Usually in these places one can not only enjoy the beauty of the natural surroundings, but also be spiritually enriched through an encounter with God through reflection and silence, through prayer and contemplation. This is a very healthy tendency, which should not remain limited to the holiday season.

It is necessary to find suitable forms so that this practice can accompany daily life also in other seasons of the year. The real problem is that of maintaining inner harmony, so that our ordinary existence always has that supernatural dimension that all of us need"

(Gratissimam sane).

In his words, the Pope mentioned the holiday season, which plays an important role in the life of the family because its members can spend more time together. This is very important today, when the whole world keeps rushing forward, when there is a hurry and constant lack of time. Everyone is busy with himself and his own affairs-school, work, the pursuit of a career... Where in all this is there time for the family? Where is the place for tightening the bonds with loved ones, creating a true community? Therefore, it is all the more important to appreciate the time off work and devote it not only to personal development and relaxation, but also to spending time together and giving of ourselves. John Paul II wrote that:

"It is necessary to use vacations and holidays wisely so that they may serve the good of the individual and the family by allowing contact with nature, by providing peace and quiet, by giving time for the cultivation of a harmonious family life, for valuable reading and for wholesome entertainment, and above

all by allowing greater devotion to prayer, contemplation and listening to the voice of God"

(Reflections, 23rd July 2000).

Of course, this doesn't mean that we should give up work or study, as they are necessary to function properly in the world. The point is to prioritize life properly and find time for what is really important and valuable. The work itself must also be dignified and care about the person as a human. The Holy Father instructs that:

"Work cannot be regarded merely as a force needed for production - so-called 'work force'. Man cannot be seen as an instrument of production. Man is the creator and producer of work. Everything must be done to ensure that work does not lose its proper dignity. For the goal of work - of all work - is man himself. Through it, he must improve himself, enhance his personality. We must not forget - and I want to emphasize this forcefully - that work is "for man" and not man "for work".

(Laborem Exercens, 1981).

Therefore:

"Great tasks are set before us by our Lord, demanding of us a testimony in the social context. As Christians, as believers, we must sensitize our consciences to every kind of injustice or form of exploitation or cover-up"

(Homily, Legnica, 2nd June 1997).
The Pope also added:

"Therefore, everything must be done to create real employment opportunities for all, while at the same time ensuring adequate remuneration for everyone. It is also necessary to provide a system of work which does not disturb the personal and family balance and does not impede the harmonious realization of the plans for the life of each person"

(Address to the participants in the ACLI Conference, April 27, 2002).

The Holy Father considers the family as the most important path in life that every human being should follow. This is because it determines the essence of our humanity and allows us to develop personally. It follows from these papal teachings that:

"Among these many paths, the family is the first and for many reasons the most important path. It is the universal way, while each time also an exceptional way, unique and unrepeatable, just as each person is unique. The family is that path from which one cannot be separated. After all, normally each of us is born into the family, so one could say that to the family one owes the very fact of being human. And if in this coming into the world and in entering the world a human being lacks the family, it is always a breach and a very disturbing, painful absence, which then weighs down on the whole life"

(Gratisssimam sane, 2).

Always and exclusively concerned with the good of the family, John Paul II has often deplored the social and cultural changes under which contemporary families find themselves. Some of them are able to be faithful to the values that constitute the foundation of the family institution, while others are not - they are lost, uncertain, doubtful. They lose the awareness of the ultimate meaning and truth of family and married life. Often at the root of these negative symptoms is a misconception and misexperience of freedom. Freedom understood as an autonomous force oriented toward the pursuit of one's own selfish good, which sometimes happens to conflict with others.

"On the one hand, there is a more lively sense of personal freedom, as well as a greater attention to the quality of interpersonal relations in marriage, to the elevation of the dignity of women, to responsible parenthood, to the upbringing of children; in addition, there is an awareness of the need to strengthen ties between families in order to provide mutual spiritual and material assistance, a fuller discovery of the ecclesial mission proper to the family and of its responsibility for building a more just society. On the other hand, however, there is no lack of worrying signs of the degradation of certain fundamental values: the theoretical and practical misconception of the independence of spouses in their relations with each other; the great confusion in the understanding of the authority of parents and children; the practical difficulties which the family often encounters in transmitting values; the ever-increasing number of divorces, the scourge of abortions, the growing recourse to sterilization; the actual perpetuation of a mentality opposed to the conception of new life"

(Familiaris consortio).

"The times in which we live reveal a tendency for the family to shrink to a bond of only two generations. This often happens as a result of housing difficulties, especially in large cities. Not unusually, however, the reason for this is the belief that more generations under one roof hinders intimacy and creates difficulties in life. But this is precisely the weakest point: there is little human life in our modern families. There is no one to create the common good with and no one to share it with. (...)

Another feature of the cultural context in which we live is the tendency of many parents to abandon their designated role and become mere friends with their children, which means that they do not admonish or reprimand them even when they should do so - with love and tenderness - in order to bring them up in truth. (Parents, however, must be the representatives in the familial community of the good Father, the only perfect model to be inspired by"

(Address to the participants in the Plenary Assembly of the of the Pontifical Council for the Family, June 4, 1999).

Christian families therefore have a great responsibility to counteract all problems and, if necessary, to solve them to the best of their ability. Otherwise, not only family communities but the whole society, nation, and even the world suffers. Let us remember the words of John Paul II, who emphasized that **through family flows the main current of the civilization of love.** *If this civilization is not to remain a utopia, then it should seek its "social foundations"* in the family (Gratissimam sane).

To sum up my reflections on the family based on papal teachings, I would like to share with you the words of the Holy Father that are particularly close to my heart:

Never forget for a moment the great value of the family.

Thanks to the sacramental presence of Christ, thanks to the vows freely given by the spouses to each other, the family is a sacred community. It is a communion of persons united by love, of which St. Paul writes that: 'love rejoices in the truth, believes all things, hopes always, endures all things, and never ceases" (cf. 1 Cor 13:6-8). Love never ceases. Every family can build such love. But it can be achieved in marriage if and only if the spouses become ... 'a selfless gift of themselves', unconditionally and forever, placing no limits.

This marital, parental, family love is constantly ennobled, it is perfected by shared concerns and joys, by supporting each other in difficult moments. It forgets itself for the sake of the loved one. True love never dies. It becomes a source of strength and marital fidelity.

The Christian family, faithful to its sacramental covenant, becomes an authentic sign of God's selfless and universal love for people. This love of God is the spiritual center of the family and its foundation. Through such love, the family arises, develops, matures and becomes a source of peace and happiness for parents and children. It is the real environment for life and love.

(Homily, Kalisz, 4th June 1997)

These words express all essential truth about the family, its essence and its duties, its foundation and spiritual center, which has its source in the love of God the Father. About the power of self-giving. About the civilization of love. About ourselves...

Therefore, *do not forget for a moment the great value of the family*. Love one another, surround yourselves with care, be supportive for one another. Create a community according to God's mission and give witness to truth, love and life. Abide - for your spouse, parents, children. Endure for all succeeding generations. Endure for the future - because *the future of humanity comes through the family...*

Child

*Caring for a child is the first
and fundamental test of
of man's relation to another.*

John Paul II

Fot. Andrzej J. Gojke

In God's design, marriage is the foundation of the broader familial community, as the very institution of marriage, and the love of spouses, are directed towards their offspring and their upbringing as its culmination. As John Paul II said:

"In its deepest reality, love is essentially a gift, and marital love, while leading the spouses to mutual familiarity that makes them 'one flesh,' does not exhaust itself among the two of them, for it empowers them to the greatest devotion by which they become God's collaborators in giving the gift of life to a new human person. In this way, by giving themselves to each other, the spouses bring forth a new reality, a child, a living reflection of their love, a permanent sign of marital unity and a living and inseparable synthesis of fatherhood and motherhood"

(Familiaris consortio).

And when the spouses become parents, they receive from God the gift of a new responsibility, for by their parental love they are to become a visible sign of that same love of God the Father for their children. From this responsibility, from this primal vocation of man and woman to share in God's work of creation, derives the task of educating their offspring. A new human being is born in love and for love, and called to grow and develop in and of themselves. The mother and father thus take on the task of making it possible for children to live a fully human life. The Second Vatican Council reminded us of this in the following words:

"Parents, because they have given life to their children, have a supreme responsibility for the upbringing of their offspring and must therefore be recognized as

their first and main educators. The duty of education is of such great importance that its lack would be difficult to replace. For it is the task of parents to create a family atmosphere imbued with love and respect for God and for humanity, in such a way as to favor the entire personal and social education of their children. For this reason the family is the first school of the social virtues indispensable to all communities".

So what is this upbringing? What does it consist of? To properly answer this question, it is impossible to ignore two fundamental truths. The first is that man has been called to live in truth and love, and the second is that each human being realizes themselves through the selfless gift of self. This applies both to those who bring up and those who are being brought up. The Holy Father wrote:

"The parents always remain first of all the immediate educators to their children. (...) they also have the first and fundamental authority in this area. They are educators because they are parents"

(Gratissimam sane).

Sometimes, however, parents, unable to meet all the educational needs (for example, a complete education or socialization), share the task of bringing up their child with other people, institutions, or the Church in accordance with the principle of subsidiarity. Subsidiarity, supported by parental love, is related to the good of the family. In this way parental love is completed and its fundamental character affirmed, especially since the other participants in the process of upbringing, act on behalf of the parents and with their consent.

This process of upbringing leads to a certain psychophysical maturity – then, man begins to "bring himself up". Here is what the Pope wrote about this phenomenon:

"As time goes on, this self-education will outgrow the previous educational process. In the course of time, this self-growth outgrows the process of upbringing, but it does not cease to grow out of it. The young person meets new people and new environments, especially teachers and schoolmates, who begin to play an educational role in his life, a positive or negative one, we might add. In this new contact there is a certain distance or even opposition to parental upbringing, to the family. In spite of everything, however, the process of self-education essentially confirms what has been accomplished in the child, boy or girl, through upbringing in the family and at school. Even as he transforms himself, as he moves away in his own direction, the young person remains in the orbit of his existential roots"

(Gratissimam sane).

Upbringing is therefore of great importance, according to the Holy Father. For it consists not only of the process of education and socialization, but also in parental love, care and concern, which are extremely important for the proper development of each little person. According to the Pope:

"In the family, as a community, particular care must be given to the child; their personal dignity must be deeply respected, and their rights must be served with reverence and generosity. This applies to every child, but

it is particularly important with regard to a small child, the child in need of full time care, a sick, suffering or handicapped child"

(Familiaris consortio).

"By caring for every child born into the world and by providing him or her with tender and attentive care, the Church fulfils her fundamental mission; she is called to reveal and to represent anew in history the example and the commandment of Christ the Lord, who placed the child at the very center of the Kingdom of God, saying: "Let the children come to me and do not prevent them from coming to me, for theirs is the kingdom of heaven"

(Familiaris consortio).

The fourth of God's commandments states: *Honor your father and your mother*. But in order for children to fulfill this commandment, they must first be considered and accepted by their parents as a gift from God. For the Holy Father believed that

"Every child is a gift from God. A gift that is sometimes difficult to accept, but always a gift that is priceless.

God has given you, the parents, a special calling. To preserve human life on earth, He has called into existence the familial community. You are the first guardians and protectors of life not yet born, but already conceived. Accept the gift of life as the greatest Grace of God, as his blessing for the family, for the nation and for the Church"

(Periodical „Miłujcie się" 2005, no 3).

John Paul II often referred to children as the springtime of the family and of society (*Address to participants in the Plenary Assembly of the Pontifical Council for the Family*, June 4, 1999) and pointed out that *great and noble is the mission of fathers and mothers, called to collaborate with the heavenly Father in conveying life to new human beings, the children of God*". But what does the metaphor of "children are springtime" mean? The Pope addressed this question as follows:

"It introduces us to the atmosphere full of life, colors, light and singing that we associate with spring. All this is naturally present in children. Children are the hope that blossoms again and again ... Coming into the world, they bring with them the message of life, which points to the first Creator of life. In everything they depend on us, especially in the early stages of life, they are a natural call to solidarity"

(*Jubilee of Families*, 14th October 2000).

The Holy Father came back to this issue many times in his speeches and writings. He claimed that:

"The joy that children represent for each of us [is] the springtime of life, the presage of the future of every homeland today. No country in the world, no political system, can think about its future except through the vision of those new generations who will take over from their parents, the heritage of a variety of values, duties, and aspirations both of their own nation and of the entire human family. (...) And therefore, what more can one wish for each nation and for all humanity, for all the children of the world, if not that better future in

which respect for human rights becomes a full reality in the coming year?"

(Familiaris consortio).

"Acceptance, love, respect, a manifold and uniform service - material, affectional, educational, spiritual - to every child who comes into this world must always constitute a characteristic and indispensable feature of Christians, and especially of Christian families, so that children, having the opportunity to grow "in wisdom, in years and in grace with God and with men", may make a valuable contribution to the building of the familial community and to the sanctification of the parents themselves"

(Familiaris Consortio).

"After all, don't children constantly put their parents to a kind of test? They do it not only by asking questions, but also by the expression on their faces, sometimes happy, sometimes sad. Their whole way of being, sometimes even their childish whims, are as if inscribed with questions, uttered in various ways, which we could read, for example, as follows: Mom and Dad, do you love me? Am I really a gift to you? Do you accept me as I am? Do you always strive for my true wellbeing?

These questions may be asked more with the eyes than with words, but they make parents aware of their great responsibility and echo God's voice"

(Jubilee of Families, 14th October 2000)

The Holy Father also pointed out that children are open and sincere in their intentions, that they have great power of communication, that they can be guides also for adult people. He wrote, among other things:

"What immense power the prayer of a child has! It sometimes becomes a model for adults: to pray with simplicity and complete trust, that is to address God as children do"

(Letter to children, Tra pochi giorno, 13th December 1994).

Therefore, not only can children learn from adults, but adults can also learn a lot from children. However, this does not change the fact that it is the parents' mission to guide the destiny of their children. For as John Paul II said:

"In this reflection you also cannot avoid the fundamental question of your educational mission. Since you have given life to your children, you also have the duty to help them, in a way appropriate to their age, to choose their path and to make their decisions in life while respecting all of their rights"

(Jubilee of Families, 14th October 2000).

The **educational mission of parents** is also important in the context of the country, as it is the mother and father who instill patriotism, loyalty, the idea of sacrifice and service to the nation in the child.

"Let us try to develop and deepen in the hearts of children and young people patriotic feelings and a bond with the homeland. Sensitize them to the common good of the nation and teach them responsibility for the future.

Raising the young generation in the spirit of love of the homeland is of great importance for the future of the nation. For one cannot serve the nation well without knowing its history, rich tradition and culture. Poland needs people who are open to the world, but who love their home country"

(Homily, Łowicz, 14th June 1999).

John Paul II also often spoke directly to children and young people, and he loved both to joke with them and to talk about various important subjects. In one of his speeches, he asked children experiencing their First Holy Communion to pray for their peers experiencing multiple sufferings:

"Dear friends, your First Holy Communion is undoubtedly an unforgettable meeting with Our Lord Jesus. It is a day remembered as one of the most beautiful in life. It is a great celebration for the family. It is also a great celebration in the parish. I still remember that day when I received the Eucharist for the first time in my parish church, among my peers. I would like to entrust to your prayers, dear little friends, not only the affairs of your family, but of all families in the world. The Pope counts very much on your prayers. We must pray together so that humanity - and there are many billions of people on Earth - may become more and more the family of God, so that they may live in peace. Many children in various parts of the world suffer and are threatened in many ways. They suffer hunger and poverty, die of disease and malnutrition, become victims of war, are abandoned by their parents, condemned to

homelessness, deprived of the warmth of their families, and subjected to various forms of rape and violence by adults. Can one be indifferent to the suffering of so many children?"
(Letter to Children in the Year of the Family, 13th December 1994).

For many children, the time of the First Holy Communion is the moment of joining the Pontifical Missionary Work, in which John Paul II, as well as his successors Benedict XVI and Francis, recognized one of the most beautiful paths to friendship with Jesus. Importantly, it does not end with the removal of the communion garment, but deepens and strengthens over the years.

John Paul II also referred to values in his speeches to young people. He pointed out to them the path they should follow:

"Each of you, young friends, also finds in life some kind of his 'Westerplatte'. Some dimension of duties that must be undertaken and fulfilled. There is a righteous cause for which it is impossible not to fight. Some duty, obligation which one cannot evade. You cannot desert"
(Homily, Westerplatte, 12th June 1987)

The Holy Father showed great love for children and young people, he surrounded them with care, he prayed for them, their fate was always in his heart. Therefore, as a conclusion to this part of our reflections, I would like to quote the words of John Paul II about children, with which I fully agree with:

"Children are a hope that blossoms again and again, a project that continually materializes a future that

always remains open. They are the fruit of marital love, which, thanks to them, is continually revived and strengthened"

(Homily, Vatican, 14th October 2000).

What more can be said...? Children are the future of the world - they are our future.

Senior

Old age is the final stage of human maturity and a sign of God's blessing.

(Letter to the Elderly, 1999)

In his teaching about life and old age, John Paul II put great emphasis on the dignity and the value of old age, and thus on the mission of the elderly. In his case, these were not just words, but confirmed by his own personal example, especially at the stage when he himself was living through his old age, and yet did not renounce the service of God until the end, in order to finally pass from earthly to eternal life, to which he opened himself with inextinguishable Christian hope.

The pope emphasized that an elderly person has the same dignity as created and redeemed by God as other people:

"At the same time however man is set apart from all other realities around him, precisely because he is a person. Made in the image and likeness of God, he is conscious and responsible"

(Letter to the Elderly,
Vatican, 1st October 1999).

From the Christian point of view, even in old age being human means much more than any wealth or human achievements or works. In his speeches, the Holy Father proclaimed with conviction what his other writings also affirmed:

"According to the divine plan, each individual human being lives a life of continual growth, from the beginning of existence to the moment at which the last breath is taken"

(Christifideles Laici).

Therefore, this is the spirit in which the education of the young generation should be conducted – with respect for the dignity and personal integrity of the elderly. John Paul II exhorted that:

> *"Such policies also need to be complemented by lifelong educational programmes intended to prepare people for old age, enabling them to adapt to changes in life-style and work, which occur ever more rapidly. This will need to be a formation centred not upon «doing» but above all on «being», with a focus on the values which help people to make the best use of their life in all its phases, through the acceptance of both its possibilities and its limitations.(…)*
>
> *To address the fact of ageing therefore means taking account of the human person who, from birth till death, is a gift of God, his image and imprint. It means to be resolute in ensuring that every moment of human life is lived in dignity and fullness"*
>
> (Letter to the President of the Second World Assembly on Ageing, Vatican, 3rd April 2002).

In general, the Pope wanted to sensitize the younger generation to the fact that every person, regardless of age, is a human being, equally worthy of care.

> *"What is in question here is man in all his truth, in his full magnitude. We are not dealing with "abstract" man, but the real, "concrete", "historical" man. We are dealing with "each" man, for each one is included in the mystery of the Redemption and with each one Christ has united himself for ever through this mystery. Every man comes into the world through being conceived in his mother's womb and being born of his mother, and precisely because of the mystery of the Redemption is entrusted to the solicitude of the Church. Her solicitude*

is about the whole man and is focussed on him in an altogether special manner. The object of her care is man in his unique unrepeatable human reality, which keeps intact the image and likeness of God himself"

(Redemptor hominis).

John Paul II pointed out that the full extent of our humanity is evidenced precisely by our respect for others and our ability to give ourselves to them. He asked:

"In this way therefore we learn to know other human beings, in order to become more fully human through our capacity for "self giving": for becoming men and women "for others" . This truth about man-this anthropology-has its incomparable culmination in Jesus of Nazareth"

(Apostolic Letter Dilecti Amici to the Youth of the World on the Occasion of International Youth Year, 1985).

Referring to the Holy Scriptures, in his teachings the Holy Father said:

"The word of God frequently repeats the call to show care and respect, above all where life is undermined by sickness and old age. Although there are no direct and explicit calls to protect human life at its very beginning, specifically life not yet born, and life nearing its end, this can easily be explained by the fact that the mere possibility of harming, attacking, or actually denying life in these circumstances is completely foreign to the religious and cultural way of thinking of the People of God"

(Evangelium Vitae).

We see, therefore, how often the Pope referred in his texts and speeches to the subject of old age, how deeply he cared about the elderly, emphasizing the need to protect and care for them. Referring to the papal teachings of John Paul II, father Wieslaw Przygoda in his work entitled "The Apostolic Formation of the Elderly" also raises the issue of old age. He states that it is not the number of years that determines it, but a significant decrease in the biological and psychosocial aspect of human adaptive abilities. It is related to progressive reduction of life independence and gradual intensification of dependence on other people. Very often it is also accompanied by a feeling of rejection, of being disposable. Nothing could be further from the truth!

Senior citizens have always been and will always will be important.

John Paul II emphasized this many times in his speeches. According to the Pope, old age appears as:

> "(…) a "favourable time" for bringing life to its fulfilment and, in God's plan for each person, as a time when everything comes together and enables us better to grasp life's meaning and to attain "wisdom of heart". "An honourable old age comes not with the passing of time", observes the Book of Wisdom, "nor can it be measured in terms of years; rather, understanding is the hoary crown for men, and an unsullied life, the attainment of old age" (4:8-9). Old age is the final stage of human maturity and a sign of God's blessing"
>
> (Letter to the Elderly, Vatican, 1st October 1999).

The Holy Father wrote not about the shadows of old age, but about its brightness, not about the dependence of older people on the younger, but about the interdependence between generations, which is the foundation of community. In a passage from the above-mentioned letter, he expressed the view that:

"(…) the signs of human frailty which are clearly connected with advanced age become a summons to the mutual dependence and indispensable solidarity which link the different generations, inasmuch as every person needs others and draws enrichment from the gifts and charisms of all".

In the past, it seemed obvious that adult children would naturally surround their parents with care and concern. According to the Holy Father, the family then fulfilled a basic form of intergenerational solidarity, based on several stages. Initially, marital solidarity meant that spouses bound themselves to each other for better or for worse, thus committing themselves to care for each other until the end of their days. Then this solidarity extended to the offspring, because raising children requires a strong and enduring bond between the mother and the father. Finally, there was solidarity between adult children and their aging parents. Is this still the case?

"At present relations between generations are undergoing significant changes as a result of various factors. In many areas there has been a weakening of the marriage bond, which is often perceived as a mere contract between two individuals. The pressures of a consumer society can cause families to divert attention from the home to the workplace or to a variety of social activities"

(Address to the Members of the Pontifical Academy of Social Sciences, 30th April 2004).

Today, the position of the elderly in the family depends primarily on the values recognized by the community. Thus, where experience and wisdom are valued, senior citizens are treated with care, kindness and respect. On the other hand, where youth and productivity are valued, older people are treated as a burden and pushed to the margins of social life. John Paul II was very proud of this first group.

"There are cultures which manifest a unique veneration and great love for the elderly: far from being outcasts from the family or merely tolerated as a useless burden, they continue to be present and to take an active and responsible part in family life, though having to respect the autonomy of the new family; above all they carry out the important mission of being a witness to the past and a source of wisdom for the young and for the future"

(Familiaris consortio, 27).

The Holy Father emphasized that relegating the elderly to the margins of social life is not only a source of their suffering, but also spiritually impoverishes the modern family. He argued that «respect and love for the elderly, due to which they can - despite their weakening strength – feel like a living part of society» are necessary for the proper functioning of any community. Older people serve younger people with their experience, advice and wisdom, and therefore, according to the Pope, deserve not only their respect, but even their admiration. We even find here a reference to God's fourth commandment: «honor your father and your mother.»

According to John Paul II:

"Honouring older people involves a threefold duty: welcoming them, helping them and making good use

of their qualities. In many places this happens almost spontaneously, as the result of long-standing custom. (…) Older people can give you much more than you can imagine"

(Letter to the Elderly,
Vatican, 1st October 1999).

Thus, according to the Holy Father, reverence towards the elderly should be manifested in the family by accepting their presence, helping them and appreciating their qualities. This allows us to see the wisdom of the elderly, from which the young can benefit as a treasury of knowledge and experience. In the above mentioned letter the Pope also wrote that:

"As Saint Jerome observes, with the quieting of the passions, it [old age] "increases wisdom, and brings more mature counsels" (…) In a certain sense, it is the season for that wisdom which generally comes from experience, since "time is a great teacher".

Therefore, John Paul II pointed out that the Church of Christ, in her teaching on the wisdom of old age, also remembers the extremely valuable role of older people in the family. He pointed out that:

"The Church cannot ignore the time of old age, with all its positive and negative aspects. In old age married love, which has been increasingly purified and ennobled by long and unbroken fidelity, can be deepened. There is the opportunity of offering to others, in a new form, the kindness and the wisdom gathered over the years, and what energies remain. (…) There is also suffering

caused by ill-health, by the gradual loss of strength, by the humiliation of having to depend on others, by the sorrow of feeling that one is perhaps a burden to one's loved ones, and by the approach of the end of life"

(Familiaris consortio 1981).

According to the Holy Father, in old age there is hidden the wisdom of life, the richness of experience and the simple maturity of a man who can see more.

"(…) Genuine intellectual maturity always goes hand in hand with simplicity. The latter does not consist in a superficiality of life and thought nor in denial of the problematic nature of reality, but rather in knowing how to go to the heart of every question and to discover its essential meaning and relationship to the whole. Simplicity is wisdom"

(Homily, Vatican, 23rd October 1998).

John Paul II explained many times the value of the elderly:

"Elderly people help us to see human affairs with greater wisdom, because life's vicissitudes have brought them knowledge and maturity. They are the guardians of our collective memory, and thus the privileged interpreters of that body of ideals and common values which support and guide life in society"

(Letter to the Elderly, Vatican, 1st October 1999).

It seems so obvious once it is pointed out.

Senior

Norbet Pikuła brilliantly describes in his dissertation on "The Life Wisdom of Elderly People as an Educational Paradigm for the Modern Family" - After all, it is grandma and grandpa who most often teach the words of the trowel and provide assistance in basic schooling. They pass on their sacred values and in this way shape the attitudes of the youngest. They are a spiritual support for their children and grandchildren. They are happy to tell both beautiful fairy tales and true stories which they themselves often witnessed. They share their knowledge about family and national celebrations, and they uphold the traditions of experiencing holidays or important national dates in the life of their homeland. They are the living testaments to history.

Therefore, emphasizing the wisdom of the elderly, John Paul II said to the senior citizens:

"You are a blessing to the world. How often you have to relieve the young parents, how well you can introduce the little ones to the history of your family and your homeland, to the tales of your nation and to the world of faith! Young people more often turn to you with their problems than to their parents' generation"

(Speech to the Elderly,
Munich, 19th November 1980).

> "Old age too has a proper role to play in this process of gradual maturing along the path to eternity. And this process of maturing cannot but benefit the larger society of which the elderly person is a part"
>
> (Letter to the Elderly, Vatican, 1ˢᵗ October 1999).

John Paul II also pointed out that the relationship between the elderly and the family should be seen as an exchange of gifts. Just as the family is a true "sanctuary of life and love," its members are a gift to one another.

> "In fact, "the life of the aging helps to clarify a scale of human values; it shows the continuity of generations and marvelously demonstrates the interdependence of God's people. The elderly often have the charism to bridge generation gaps before they are made: how many children have found understanding and love in the eyes and words and caresses of the aging!"
>
> (Familiaris consortio).

When it comes to the relationship between seniors and young people, the Holy Father also said:

> "They can serve them with their discreet and cordial kindness, wisdom, understanding, patience, good advice, and especially with their faith and prayers".

John Paul II emphasized that old age is not a disease, but a natural period of every person's life.

> "I now address older people, oftentimes unjustly

considered as unproductive, if not directly an insupportable burden. I remind older people that the Church calls and expects them to continue to exercise their mission in the apostolic and missionary life. This is not only a possibility for them, but it is their duty even in this time in their life when age itself provides opportunities in some specific and basic way"

(Christifideles Laici 1988).

According to John Paul II, the mission of the elderly is essentially to bear witness "to true values whose meaning goes beyond appearances and which endure forever because they are inscribed in the heart of every man and vouched for by the word of God." In his letter to the elderly (1999), he wrote that the peculiar evangelizing task of the elderly is the apostolate of prayer. He also believed that the privilege of the elderly is time, as they are no longer distracted by numerous activities and can "foster deeper reflection and a longer dialogue with God". This is the same time to which man is subject, being born in him and then passing away.

There is also nothing new in saying that the Holy Father identified with seniors for almost the entire period of his pontificate. He repeatedly emphasized his age and understanding of the problems of this group. Among other things, he wrote as follows:

"In speaking to the elderly, I know I am speaking to and about people who have made a long journey (cf. Wis 4:13). I am speaking to my contemporaries, and so I can readily draw an analogy from my own personal experience.

As an older person myself, I have felt the desire to engage in a conversation with you. I do so first of all by thanking God for the gifts and the opportunities which he has abundantly bestowed upon me up to now. In my memory I recall the stages of my life, which is bound up with the history of much of this century, and I see before me the faces of countless people, some particularly dear to me: they remind me of ordinary and extraordinary events, of happy times and of situations touched by suffering. Above all else, though, I see outstretched the provident and merciful hand of God the Father, who "cares in the best way possible for all that exists" and who "hears us whenever we ask for anything according to his will" (1 Jn 5:14)"

(Letter to the Elderly,
Vatican, 1st October 1999).

The Pope's entire reflection on old age, however, boils down to gratitude:

"There are many reasons, then, for giving thanks to God. All things considered, these final years of our century present immense potential for peace and progress. From the very adversities which our generation has experienced there comes a light which can brighten the years of our old age"

(Letter to the Elderly,
Vatican, 1st October 1999).

Referring to the words of the Holy Father, John Paul II, confirmed by his experience, we can not only learn the deepest sense of old age and the irreplaceable mission of seniors, but also strengthen their social relevance both in the family and social environment. From the power of the testimony of his word and life, remains the call to contemporary people and communities to reach for a credible, authentic affirmation of the dignity of man in old age, and for the resulting social imperatives.

Just as children are the future of the world, the elderly are the guarantee of its permanence and continuity. Therefore, let us take care of them - let us take care of ourselves...

A beloved motto of mine states:

An elderly person is like a beautifully written book. When a person dies, a library dies with them.

Fot. Janusz Gojke

A few more anecdotes from the life of Saint John Paul II

Glass cage

The Pope was very unhappy with the fact that he was being driven around in a glass cage. This idea was defended by a Polish woman who, having had the opportunity to speak with John Paul II in Krakow, said:

'But this cage reduces the risk, after all. We can't help feeling anxious for Your Holiness.'

'Me too', smiled the Pope, 'I am anxious about my holiness'.

I become childish around you

During one of his visits to Rome's parishes, the Pope, as was his custom, got into a conversation with children.

'You are young and I am old', he said.

'No, you are not old', the children protested loudly.

'I am, but I become childish around you', the Pope replied.

Call me uncle

During his first visit to the United States, the Pope met with the family of President Jimmy Carter. The president's then five-year-old granddaughter, having trouble articulating her greeting, repeated over and over:

'His Holiness, His Holiness...'

The Pope, wanting to save the little girl from trouble, took her in his arms and said:

'Just call me uncle.'

He was also a teacher

It was the winter exam session. The students were waiting for Prof. Karol Wojtyla, who was to examine them in ethics. After two hours they all went home, except for one student, a priest who had not attended a single lecture by Prof. Wojtyla during the whole semester because instead he was travelling for painting exhibitions in Warsaw.

The professor priest came straight from the delayed train to the examination room. He looked very young and did not stand out visually among the student priests who were only a few years younger than him. The student priest asked K. Wojtyla, whom he had never seen before:

- Hey man, are you here for the exam too?

The student priest began to lament the examiner's tardiness, and the examiner immediately realized that the person waiting had not attended his lectures. He sat down next to him and they began an hour-long conversation related to the ethical issues that were the subject of the lectures. The student priest looked at Father Wojtyla with admiration and said:

'Man, you're so well prepared! Please, if the professor comes, don't enter the exam before me because in comparison I'll will surely fail!'

'All right', agreed Father Wojtyla humbly, 'but tell me honestly, why haven't you been to a single lecture?'

'You know, the general opinion is that his lectures are very difficult and even abstract, but if he had such a gift of passing knowledge as you, I would listen to him with the greatest pleasure.'

'Alright then, give me your record book', said the professor.

'What are you, kidding me?' the priest asked, to which he heard the answer:

'I am Wojtyla.'

And the professor gave the terrified student his grade (4+), with a remark that he should start attending lectures next semester to make up his own mind about the lecturer. With this admittedly small event, which the other students learned about immediately, he gained such sympathy that the barrier of illusory fear was conquered forever.

The Pope is not an olympic champion

Vatican employees couldn't get over the fact that the new pope did not want to use the papal lectern, called a *sedia gestatoria*.

'Without the *sedia gestatoria* His Holiness will not be seen, so how about some platform?', the Vatican staff did not give up.

'I will not go up on the platform, I am not an Olympic champion!', said John Paul II firmly.

Fot. Andrzej J. Gojke

John Paul II Trivia

1. Karol Wojtyla was the first non-Italian pope since 1522, and of course the first Slav to hold the office of the Pope. He was Pope for 26 years.

2. Karol Wojtyla was barely just in time for the conclave at which he was elected Pope! He was the last to enter the Sistine Chapel, and it should be mentioned that after the gates are closed no one is allowed in, not even cardinals.

3. Karol Wojtyla was born at the same time of day as he was elected Pope - that is, between 5 and 6 p.m. but 58 years earlier.

4. John Paul II made 104 foreign pilgrimages, including 9 to Poland. He visited as many as 129 countries of the world and more than 900 cities and towns. His great dream was to go on pilgrimages to Orthodox Russia and China, but it never happened.

5. During all his foreign trips John Paul II traveled more than 1,650,900 km, which is equivalent to 30 times around the Earth (along the equator) and 3 times the distance between the Earth and the Moon.

6. John Paul II was physically active and loved sports. He enjoyed skiing and canoeing, and he loved mountain climbing. In the first year of his pontificate, he asked the government to build a swimming pool and to renovate the tennis court.

7. John Paul II gave up the lectern in which popes had been carried until then. He felt that it was completely unnecessary, and he himself did not want to be carried around.

8. John Paul II broke all stereotypes. He was the first Pope to attend a rock concert (in Bologna). He was also the first Pope to give audiences in the media, which over time were transformed into press conferences.

9. John Paul II is famous for introducing the internet to the Vatican, an incredible undertaking previously unattainable for inhabitants of the Vatican city.

10. The Pope was also a very unusual person, he wore a watch on his wrist and read without glasses. He often joked and talked about his preferences - for example, he was very fond of the Wadowice cream cake, which he used to enjoy with his friends after his high school graduation.

11 John Paul II loved children very much, he always wanted these innocent beings to have a good and decent life. He was also the first Pope to write a letter addressed specifically to children.

12. John Paul II was also the first Pope to speak so many foreign languages. He was fluent in seven: English, German, French, Italian, Spanish, Portuguese, Polish, Russian, Ukrainian, Czech, Hungarian and Latin.

13. During his pontificate John Paul II beatified 1338 people and canonized 487 people.

14. John Paul II was the 264th Pope in succession (counting from St. Peter) in the history of the Church.

15. John Paul II convened 15 synods of bishops, which he personally presided over, as well as 6 extraordinary consistories of cardinals to discuss important matters. He made 14 encyclicals, 15 exhortations, 11 apostolic constitutions, and 45 apostolic letters, as well as several series of messages: for World Day of Peace (27), for World Day of the Sick (13), World Youth Day (20), World Day of the Media (26), as well as for Christmas, Lent, and Easter. In addition, he gave several cycles of catechesis as part of his Wednesday audiences. As Pope, he also published 5 books.

John Paul II – selected quotes

The crisis of civilisation should be countered
with a civilisation of love
(Tertio millennio adveniente, 1994)

*For man becomes truly himself through
becoming a free gift of himself*
(Centesimus annus, 1991)

A man must be measured by the measure of his heart.
His heart! (...)
Man must be measured by the measure of conscience,
by the measure of his spirit's openness to God.
(1979)

God does not doubt about man.
So we as Christians cannot doubt about man either, for we know
that man is always greater than his errors and transgressions.
*(Apostolic Letter for the 50th anniversary of
the outbreak of World War II, 1989)*

Man realizes himself through his intelligence and his freedom,
and in doing so, he treats them as objects and
instruments of the things of this world
and appropriates them.
(Centesimus annus, 1991)

The man who wants to fully understand himself
must come closer to Christ – with his anxiety, his insecurities,
his weakness and sinfulness,
with his life and his death.
(Redemptor hominis, 1979)

Katarzyna Dorosz

Indeed, man's greatest wealth, along with the earth, is man himself.
(Cenesimus annus, 1991)

May your Spirit come and renew the face of the land.
This land!
(Homily at Victory Square, 2nd June 1979)

Modern man is threatened by spiritual numbness,
and even the death of conscience.

Do not be afraid, do not be dismayed! Venture out into the deep!

There is no peace without justice,
there is no justice without forgiveness.

When the going gets tough,
when you experience some failure or disappointment in your life,
let your thoughts run to Christ
who loves you,
who is a faithful companion
and who helps you through every difficulty.

A family strong in God
becomes the strength of a person and of a nation.

Have high expectations of yourselves, even if
others place no expectations on you.

Love has explained everything to me,
Love has solved everything -
so I love this Love,
wherever it may be...

(from The Renaissance Psalter)

I was looking for you, now you have found me.

You are the future of the world!
You are the hope of the Church!
You are my hope!

Caring for children is the first and fundamental test
of man's relationship with another.

The rich are not those who possess, but those who give.

Be bearers of Christian faith and hope in this world,
Live in love every day.
Be faithful witnesses of the resurrected Christ,
never retreat from the obstacles that stand in your way.
I am counting on you. On your youthful
enthusiasm and devotion to Christ.

It is never the case that a man, in doing good to another,
becomes only the benefactor.
He is at the same time receiving a gift,
bestowed with what the other one accepts with love.
Let us try to act and live this way,
So that no one in our Homeland lacks a roof
over their head and bread on the table,
so that no one feels lonely and left without care.

You are young and the Pope is old and a little tired.
But he still identifies with your expectations and hopes.

(at World Youth Day, 28th July 2002)

Man is not only the author of his acts,
but through these acts in some way he
also becomes his own creator.

You pay for freedom with your whole self
- so call it freedom
that you can, by paying this price again
and again, be your own master.

(Memory and Identity)

Bibliografia

Materiały źródłowe:

Jan Paweł II, Adhortacja *Familiaris Consortio*, 1981
Jan Paweł II, Adhortacja *Christifideles Laici*, 1988
Jan Paweł II, Adhortacja *Ecclesia in Europa*, 2003
Jan Paweł II, Encyklika *Redemptor hominis*, 1979
Jan Paweł II, Encyklika *Centesimus annus*, 1991
Jan Paweł II, Encyklika *Veritatis Splendor*, 1993
Jan Paweł II, Encyklika *Evangelium vitae*, 1995
Jan Paweł II, Homilia, Watykan, 1981
Jan Paweł II, Homilia, Wrocław 1983
Jan Paweł II, Homilia, Lyon, 1986
Jan Paweł II, Homilia dla świata pracy, Gdańsk, 1987
Jan Paweł II, Homilia, Kielce, 1991
Jan Paweł II, Homilia, Skoczów, 1995
Jan Paweł II, Homilia, Kalisz, 1997
Jan Paweł II, Homilia, Legnica, 1997
Jan Paweł II, Homilia, Watykan, 1998
Jan Paweł II, Homilia, Łowicz, 1999
Jan Paweł II, Homilia, Sandomierz, 1999
Jan Paweł II, Homilia, Sopot, 1999
Jan Paweł II, Homilia, Stary Sącz, 1999
Jan Paweł II, Homilia, Watykan, 2000
Jan Paweł II, Kazanie podczas mszy św. z okazji Jubileuszu Rodzin, 2000
Jan Paweł II, List apostolski *Salvici doloris*, 1984
Jan Paweł II, List apostolski z okazji 50 rocznicy wybuchu II wojny światowej, 1989
Jan Paweł II, List apostolski *Tertio millennio adveniente*, 1994
Jan Paweł II, List apostolski *Mulieris dignitatem*, 1994

Jan Paweł II, List apostolski *Novo millennio inuente*, 2001
Jan Paweł II, List do dzieci w Roku Rodziny, 1994
Jan Paweł II, List do Équipes Notre-Dame, 1997
Jan Paweł II, List do osób w podeszłym wieku, Watykan, 1999
Jan Paweł II, List do rodzin *Gratissimam Sane*, 1988
Jan Paweł II, List do uczestników II Światowego Zgromadzenia poświęconego problemom starzenia się ludzi, Watykan, 2002
Jan Paweł II, List do uczestników sesji plenarnej Papieskiej Akademii Nauk Społecznych, 2004
Jan Paweł II, List przesłany na IV Światową Konferencję ONZ poświęconą Kobiecie, 1995
Jan Paweł II, *Miłość jest darem z samego siebie. Rozważanie przed modlitwą niedzielną*, 1994
Jan Paweł II, *Musicie od siebie wymagać*, „Miłujcie się" 2005, Nr 3
Jan Paweł II, Orędzie na XXVIII Światowy Dzień Pokoju, Watykan, 1994
Jan Paweł II, Przemówienie do młodzieży akademickiej zgromadzonej przed kościołem św. Anny, 1979
Jan Paweł II, Przemówienie podczas spotkania z młodzieżą, Jasna Góra, 1983
Jan Paweł II, Przemówienie do ludzi starych, Monachium, 1980
Jan Paweł II, Przemówienie do uczestników zgromadzenia plenarnego Papieskiej Rady ds. Rodziny, 1999
Jan Paweł II, Przemówienie z okazji Jubileuszu Rodzin, 2000
Jan Paweł II, Przemówienie podczas beatyfikacji Marii i Alozjego Quattrocchi, 2001
Jan Paweł II, Przemówienie do uczestników konferencji ACLI, 2002
Jan Paweł II, Przemówienie podczas Światowych Dni Młodzieży, 2002
Jan Paweł II, Przemówienie Papieża do uczestników zgromadzenia plenarnego Papieskiej Rady ds. Rodziny, 2004
Jan Paweł II, Rozważanie, 2000
Jan Paweł II, Rozważanie, 2002

Jan Paweł II, *Teologia małżeństwa*, Katechezy wygłoszone przez papieża w czasie audiencji środowych w latach 1979-1984, http://www.madel.jezuici.pl/ rodzina/Jan-Pawel-II-Teologia-malzenstwa.html

Paweł VI, Encyklika *Humanae vitae*, 1968

Paweł VI, Konstytucja duszpasterska *Gaudium et spes*, 1965

Sobór Watykański II, Konstytucja dogmatyczna *Lumen gentium*, 1964

Literatura przedmiotu:

Bronk K., *Franciszek potwierdza nauczanie Jana Pawła II o rodzinie*, Vatican News, 31.10.2019, https://www.vaticannews.va/pl/papiez/news/2019-10/pa piez-franciszek-jan-pawel-ii-rodzina--nauczanie.html

Bujak A., Wojtyła K., *Renesansowy psałterz*, Kraków 1999

Brzeziński M. (Ks.), *O czci i szacunku wobec ludzi starszych na kanwie listu do osób w podeszłym wieku Jana Pawła II*, „Roczniki Nauk o Rodzinie i Pracy Socjalnej" 2012, Nr 4 (59)

Chmielewski M. (Ks.), *Duchowość według Jana Pawła II. Studium na podstawie encyklik i adhortacji*, Lublin 2013

Chmielewski M. (Ks.), *Medytacyjny wymiar „Geniuszu kobiety". Refleksja nad Listem apostolskim „Mulieris dignitatem"*, „Ateneum Kapłańskie" 1994, Nr 86

Kroczek P. (Ks.), *List do rodzin Gratissimam Sane jako wskazówka dla prawodawstwa państwowego*, Kraków 2015

Kupczak P., *Wolność osoby ludzkiej według Karola Wojtyły – Jana Pawła II*, „Teologia w Polsce" 2011, Nr 5, 1

Lubowicki K., *Duchowość małżeńska w nauczaniu Jana Pawła II*, Kraków 2012

Pikuła N., *Mądrość życiowa osób starszych paradygmatem wychowawczym współczesnej rodziny*. W: B. Balogová (red.), *Elan vital v priestore medzigeneracnych vztahov*, Presov 2010

Opiela M., *Jan Paweł II słowem i życiem o starości i posłannictwie osób w podeszłym wieku*, Rozprawy Społeczne 2015, Nr 4 (IX)

Półtawska W., *By rodzina była Bogiem silna*, Częstochowa 2003

Przygoda W. (Ks.), *Formacja apostolska ludzi w podeszłym wieku*, „Legnickie Studia Teologiczno-Historyczne Perspectiva" 2009, Nr 1 (14)

Syczewski Tadeusz (Ks.), *Myśl Jana Pawła II o małżeństwie i rodzinie*, Materiały dla studentów, https://www.kul.pl/files/1418/materialy_na_zajecia/syczewski/ mysl_jana_pawla_ii_o_malzenstwie-_i_rodzinie.doc+&cd=1&hl=pl&ct=clnk&gl=pl

Szymecki S. (Abp), *Jan Paweł II*, „Czas Miłosierdzia" 2003, Nr 6

Wojtyła K. (Kard.), *Osoba i czyn oraz inne studia antropologiczne*, Lublin 2019

Wuwer A. (Ks.), *Drogi Kościoła prowadzą do człowieka*, „Gość Niedzielny" 2001, Nr 29

Substantive consultation and correction:
Katarzyna Królewicz-Gorzelańczyk

Graphic composition of the book:
Łukasz Bieszke

Cover AKSiM

Photos:
Andrzej J. Gojke, Janusz Gojke,
National Digital Archives,

The painting on the 2nd side is by the painter Robert Kraszewski

ISBN - 978-1-0879-9129-0

This edition is copyright © 2021 by Katarzyna Dorosz

All rights reserved. No part of this book
may be published or copied without written permission.

Table of Contents

Introduction
-5-

From his mentor
-18-

Ecce Homo
-29-

Woman
-45-

Man
-63-

Marriage
-73-

Family
-97-

Child
-119-

Senior
-131-

Fot. Janusz Gojke

www.ingramcontent.com/pod-product-compliance
Lightning Source LLC
LaVergne TN
LVHW010216070526
838199LV00062B/4610